Girl Mogul

DREAM IT. DO IT. CHANGE THE WORLD.

tiffany pham

{Imprint}
MAKE YOUR MARK

New York

For my loving family.
For our amazing team.
And for all the young girls around the world
who want to believe in themselves.
The underdogs.

THIS IS FOR YOU.

[Imprint]
MAKE YOUR MARK

A part of Macmillan Publishing Group, LLC
175 Fifth Avenue, New York, NY 10010

GIRL MOGUL: DREAM IT. DO IT. CHANGE THE WORLD. Copyright © 2019 by Tiffany Pham All rights reserved.
All photographs © copyright Tiffany Pham unless otherwise noted.
Printed in China by Toppan Leefung Printing Ltd., Dongguan City, Guangdong Province.

Cover photograph by Audrey Stimpson.
Styling by Kristin Dedorsen. Makeup and hair by Ruth Fernandez.

Library of Congress Control Number: 2018944962

ISBN 978-1-250-29896-6 (hardcover) / ISBN 978-1-250-29897-3 (ebook)

Our books may be purchased in bulk for promotional, educational, or business use.
Please contact your local bookseller or the Macmillan Corporate and Premium Sales Department at
(800) 221-7945 ext. 5442 or by email at MacmillanSpecialMarkets@macmillan.com.

Book design by Natalie C. Sousa

Imprint logo designed by Amanda Spielman

First edition, 2019

1 3 5 7 9 10 8 6 4 2

fiercereads.com

Buy this book. (And do feel free to lend!)
Borrow it from library or friend.
But moguls who steal
Will find it unreal
How quickly their businesses end.

table of contents

INTRODUCTION

No matter where in the world you sit as you read this book, I want you to know one thing:

There are no ceilings to your success.

There are no limits to what you can accomplish. You are smart, you are powerful, and you are capable of doing things that may not seem possible. With hard work, they *are* actually possible.

there are no limits

And it does not matter how old you are. There's no reason to wait to pursue success and significance. You can start today. You can take each moment of your life and seize the opportunity within it. Every day holds an invitation to start dreaming, start doing, and start changing the world.

Malala Yousafzai was only fifteen years old when she stood up for her right to an education, putting her very life at risk. At seventeen, she earned the Nobel Peace Prize for the work she does on behalf of girls, not only in her native country, Pakistan, but all over the world.

Or think about the courageous teenagers from Parkland, Florida, who spoke up after a devastating school shooting and began leading the United States in the call for change in gun control laws.

You are capable of so much. Whether your aim is to become a doctor, a politician, an artist, a singer, a teacher, or an entrepreneur, you were born to become something great. It is all within you: more power and creativity than you could ever imagine.

This book will show you how to access all the amazingness that is already inside you.

I know from my own life that the path to your future can start early. I always had big dreams. They were born the day that my beloved grandmother passed away, and I vowed that I would always make her proud. I was a teen,

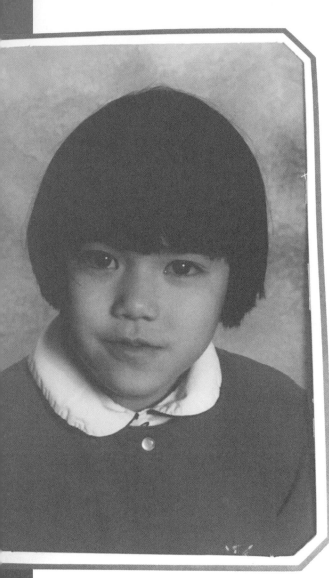

ME AT AGE SIX, A LITTLE GIRL WITH BIG DREAMS AND A BOB HAIRCUT.

and on the heels of that loss, I decided I wanted to create a company to empower women, the way that my grandmother and my parents had always empowered me. Their own lives showed me that, despite the obstacles they faced, it was possible to rise above, not to let people's stereotypes and limits confine them. At the beginning, I didn't know how I would build my company. But I worked hard with that goal in mind, every single day.

When I was twenty-seven, I built a platform for women in my bedroom. I'd come home from my full-time job and teach myself how to code between the hours of 3 A.M. and 5 A.M. After a few months of working through the night, I felt like my site was ready to share with the world. I called it **Mogul**.

It went viral in its first week.

Today, Mogul is one of the most influential companies for girls and women worldwide, reaching across 196 countries. We're everywhere—from mobile app, to web, email, social media, books, TV, films, and events globally.

We enable girls and women across

continents to connect, share knowledge, and help one another change the world. We provide access to rock-star women like Katie Couric, Chelsea Clinton, Naomi Wolf, and Rebecca Minkoff; resources to find jobs and internships at top companies; and courses on subjects like how to craft a killer résumé, how to be a successful entrepreneur, and how to manage your finances.

A **mogul** is defined in *The Oxford English Dictionary* as "an important or powerful person." But for far too long, the word was associated almost entirely with men. Just a few years ago, when you Googled the word *mogul*, the top search results were links to businessmen like Warren Buffett and Rupert Murdoch.

But today, when you Google the word *mogul*, the platform and company our team built is the number one search result. We are redefining the word *mogul* for **you**. We want you to know that you, too, are strong and important, and there is no limit to what you can do.

This book will give you the tools to step into whatever role you want to. Your training starts now. In this book, I'm going to show you how to set yourself up to succeed. While every path looks different, there are a few key components of becoming a **Girl Mogul**:

Confidence: knowing that you have within yourself what it takes to create something powerful.

Community: looking for those who can help you achieve your dreams.

Commitment: working with every ounce of your being every single day to make it happen.

So we'll begin this journey focusing on you: helping you develop the confidence to know how awesome you are, and ensuring that you take the time to truly take care of yourself. Take it from me; confidence isn't necessarily something you are born with. While some girls seem to come out of the womb assured of their worth, most of us feel insecure throughout our lives. I was a very shy girl growing up, moving from Paris, France, and landing in Plano, Texas, at ten years old. I looked very different from those around me, plus I didn't speak much English. It took several years, and a lot of awkward moments, before I finally began to feel comfortable in my own skin and confident in my abilities. But there are ways to get there faster. Confidence is like a muscle that you exercise, and when it becomes strong, it will take you further than you think. When you learn to build confidence and take care of yourself, you begin to live life on your own terms. You no longer wait around for others to grant you something you want; you know that it is up to *you* to forge the path forward.

The second part of the book reveals just how important community is to your overall success. You've got to staff your team. This means making sure that the friends you surround yourself with are the kind who build you up and push you forward, not those who drag you down and pull you back. We will talk about dating, friendships, filtering out negativity, dealing with family life, and the importance of putting positivity out in the world (because it always comes back tenfold!).

Finally, we'll look at how to commit to living a Girl Mogul life. This is where you'll set the blueprint for your future and make it happen. You'll examine your passions to determine what kind of career path will not only allow you to flourish but let you have fun as well. You'll learn how to crush it in every area of life, and how this attitude of over-delivering early on will set you up to become a mogul. You'll learn to speak up, to realize how much you have to say and how valuable your perspective really is.

Think of this book as your personal guide not just to surviving your teen years but to thriving through them. Read it from front to back; skip around to different chapters based on what you'd like help with now, and read how I overcame many of the same challenges you might be dealing with; or skip to the end of each chapter, where I offer tips on doing your best in school, laying the foundation for the future you want, and forming relationships that'll improve every part of your life. All the things you want to achieve are real possibilities with the right approach, attitude, and skill set, which is what this book aims to pass on.

I am living proof of that. And my friends are living proof of that. You'll hear from these friends throughout the book—twelve of the most powerful moguls worldwide, including Arianna Huffington, Nastia Liukin, and more. They will serve as your mentors along the way. The only difference between you and us is a few years of hard work. And to work toward your goals, you must believe you can achieve them.

I didn't know it, but there was a mogul in me all along—and there's one in you, too.

From a young age, boys are trained to be leaders, to know their worth, to raise their hands and use their voices. Girls, on the other hand, are often scolded for speaking up or asserting ourselves, inadvertently teaching us to be quiet and accommodating. We are not always encouraged to step into the inherent power we have within. There are few primers for girls aiming high.

I hope this book can be that primer for you.

After all:

you are fierce.
you are bold.
you are unique.
you are brilliant.
you are motivated.
you are driven!
you are empowering.
you are inspiring.
you are a mogul.

PART ONE

confidence

Define your life on your own terms.

CHAPTER ONE
AWAKENING YOUR AWESOMENESS

To do great things, you have to believe you are capable of them. You have to know your worth, be assured of your power, and realize you already possess an aptitude for awesomeness.

After all, confidence is the first step to awakening your inner Girl Mogul.

Without confidence, you don't know how powerful you are, how creative you are, and how much you can accomplish. I'm not talking about the kind of confidence where you walk into a room convinced that you are the most beautiful one there. I'm not talking about how you *look* at all—this has nothing to do with your weight, height, hair color, or style. It's not about who likes you or whether you're the most popular girl in school. I'm talking about the kind of confidence that comes from deep knowledge of your smarts, skills, and significance. The kind of confidence that allows you to believe that within you is the ability to learn new things, think of innovative solutions, and bring change to the world.

This chapter is all about asking yourself the question *What am I capable of*? Have you tried something you haven't done before and learned a new skill? Have you taken a risk and succeeded? I know the answer is yes. The question is, Did you notice? You've likely never taken the time to recognize that your life has been a series of trying new things and gaining new skills. It started the moment you were born! The problem is, somewhere along the way, we stop aiming high, because we are surrounded by a culture that is afraid of failure.

To be confident in your abilities, you've got to try and try and try again. There will be times that you fail. But as long as you get back up and keep going, it's not really failure. It's a chance to learn. And once you have enough successes under your belt, you realize that there is nothing you can't tackle.

It's time to awaken the awesomeness that is already inside you. And don't worry—it doesn't matter when you start.

ALWAYS A PLACE IN MY HEART FOR PARIS.

FROM AWKWARD TO AWESOME

I was born in beautiful Paris, France, the middle child of Vietnamese and Chinese parents. We spoke French and Vietnamese at home. My siblings and I wore school uniforms straight out of the Madeline books and spent our weekends exploring the Tuileries Garden. My early childhood in Paris was a wonderland of history, shopping, and food along the River Seine, full of jaw-dropping cathedrals like Notre-Dame and majestic monuments like the Eiffel Tower.

But when I was ten years old, our family moved to Plano, Texas, for my father's work. It was jarringly different from Europe, and I became the definition of the odd girl out.

I spoke little English at the time, making my inherent quietness even more pronounced and a defining characteristic in my first few years in Texas. I sat in class coloring instead of contributing anything, doodling in a dictionary instead of starting my homework. My teachers would call my parents, concerned that I wasn't making any progress. But my parents knew to give me time. They knew I would pick up the language eventually and then be able to start participating in class and making friends.

In those early months in Texas, I would come home every day after school, and await my father's arrival. He would come home from work each evening with a different movie rental from Blockbuster. Classic '90s romantic comedies like *While You Were Sleeping* and *You've Got Mail* became my de facto English lessons.

Slowly but surely, I began to emerge from the cocoon of my family and put myself out there. With my father's encouragement, I joined the school orchestra and started taking piano lessons. I trained in Taekwondo at the local dojo and, by the time I reached high school, tried out for the lacrosse team.

I was far from confident. But at least I was no longer hiding, or afraid of standing out and being ridiculed for being different. Though I may not have been as awkward anymore, I was still trying to find my awesomeness.

So how did I go from shy barely-speaks-English Tiffany, at age ten, to the young woman who runs a global technology and media company today?

Actress, author, and producer Mindy Kaling says in her book *Why Not Me?* (which is a great title and a mantra for all of us): "Confidence is like respect; you have to earn it." I couldn't say it any better. I've learned firsthand that the only way to earn confidence is to dare to do something you once thought was impossible. When you tackle a problem that seems insurmountable, when you approach someone you thought would ignore you, when you try out for something you aren't sure you'll get chosen for, you realize how capable you are. And you'll get addicted to that feeling of accomplishment. You'll begin to feel like if you work at it, nothing is impossible.

My journey to becoming the confident woman that I am today started in math class. Math was my favorite subject when I moved to America, mainly because there was no language barrier. Numbers were numbers, and equations came out the same whether in English, French, or Vietnamese. And I was good at math. With little studying, I could still earn an A– on every test or quiz.

I discovered this fact thanks to a grade-school teacher who would hold multiplication races each week. There would be dozens of equations, and whoever solved them first would quickly jog-walk up to her desk to turn in their answers. The teacher would check their work, and call out their name if they got all the answers correct. The winner would now proudly walk back up to the front of the classroom, where the teacher would present them with a small tin of Sour Patch Kids. The winner would then select their prize—one Sour Patch Kid—and head back proudly to their desk. And while I know that a single piece of candy seems like a small token, everyone in the class wanted to be the winner.

A different student would receive the Sour Patch Kid each week, and while I was always done quickly, I was never the first to submit my answers.

But one day, I just decided—I was going to do it. I felt this determination surge inside me. I knew that I was good at multiplication and that I was fast. I could do it. I could be better than I thought.

That week, I stayed laser-focused on each problem, and quickly raced through and finished. Then I jog-walked up to that desk—where I was declared the winner.

No candy ever tasted sweeter.

The next week came, and I gave myself a pep talk again. *You can do this, Tiffany. That Sour Patch Kid can be yours.* And sure enough, I jog-walked up to her desk—again first—and won that coveted prize.

I did so every week for the rest of the year. But this was about more than candy. This was about knowing how hard I'd worked, and the powerful belief that I could accomplish something I set my mind on.

I once heard about a research study on the power of positive messaging. Two groups of students of similar mathematical ability were put in two separate rooms. One group heard that they were receiving some math problems that were very difficult to solve. The other group received the same math problems but were told that they were easy. The first group was unable to solve any of the equations. The second group solved every single one.

What you tell yourself and believe you can do truly does matter.

I received another important lesson in the power of believing in yourself during my freshman year of high school, when I had a geometry teacher who asked us students to grade our peers' papers. Toward the end of class, we would switch papers with the person in front of us and grade their work while they graded ours. I was never too focused on these grades and, therefore, usually got a 92 or 93. But I often had to grade the homework of the girl who sat in front of me, Diane. I had my hand poised ready to put a red slash through any answer she got wrong. But I never had to use my pen. There was always one grade at the top of her papers: 100%.

After a few weeks of this routine, I started to wonder why I had felt so content with my 92s. Why did it suddenly feel like I was settling? As Diane kept getting perfect score after perfect score, something awakened in me. *Could I get a 100%? If I took the time to really study each night and double-check my work?*

I remembered my experience with the Sour Patch Kids. If I put in the work and believed I could do it, I bet I could get a 100%, too. Instead of breezing through my math homework, I made sure to study the lesson carefully each night and concentrate on ensuring that the answer to each question was correct.

And after a few weeks, my grades started to rise. First it was a 95. Then a 97. And then, I got my first 100.

When Diane turned around to hand me that paper, she gave me a little smile. I smiled back. I had done it. I had gotten a perfect score.

Pretty soon, I was getting 100s on every homework assignment, and every quiz, too. Diane and I became best friends, studying together after school and occasionally meeting up at the local mall on the weekends, where we had a tradition of buying "Best Friend" key chains. Diane ended up being valedictorian of our class. And though she and I attended different colleges, we stayed best friends and both ended up attending Harvard together for graduate school. Shortly after, I was a bridesmaid in her wedding, which took place inside the cylindrical MIT Chapel, decorated with geometric shapes that seem inspired by mathematical formulas. The

night before the wedding, in the midst of all the hectic preparations, Diane showed me her "Best Friend" dice key chain, which she had kept all these years.

I'm indebted to Diane, because she set before me an example of awesomeness, and of what happens when you believe in yourself and actually apply yourself to a goal. Accomplishing that goal strengthened my confidence, so that the next seemingly insurmountable task somehow didn't seem so insurmountable anymore.

Because now that I knew what it felt like to be my best, I wanted to strive for excellence in everything.

BABY STEPS CAN TAKE YOU FAR

The confidence that I cultivated in the classroom helped me aim high when I began applying to colleges. While I applied to the state university system, I also applied to a number of schools that I had only ever read about, schools that I felt were out of my league.

YOUR AWESOMENESS CHECKLIST

What is one area in your life where you know you could up your game from good to excellent?

What could you begin to do today to awaken your awesomeness in that activity?

Tell one friend of your commitment to see this goal through, to build up your confidence muscle. Ask them to check in with you occasionally, as a reminder.

List three other areas that you could work on next:

1) _____

_____

2) _____

_____

3) _____

_____

I had purposely not told my parents about the applications, not wanting to disappoint them.

Then came the large envelopes.

My parents were moved to tears as I showed them each letter, one by one. I had been admitted to Yale. Stanford. Duke. Everywhere I had hoped.

Yale had especially intrigued me, because I was a huge *Gilmore Girls* fan. Rory Gilmore was a lot like me growing up. She was shy, the quiet one in any classroom, her nose always in a book. She stayed focused on her big goals, often sacrificing fun in the moment for a focus on the future. When she went on to attend Yale and run the school newspaper, meeting smart and interesting friends along the way, I dreamed of doing the same. I wanted to stretch myself, as she had, to grow in unexpected ways.

I felt fortunate that the school had granted me a full scholarship for the first three years. While my parents were overjoyed that I was being given the chance to attend such an esteemed school, I was equally happy that I had the opportunity to go without burdening my parents financially.

I sent in my acceptance check, even though I still hadn't even visited the campus. I couldn't believe I was going to build a new life in New Haven, Connecticut, and I was incredibly nervous and excited to start. Yet when I walked onto campus, I felt like a total outsider. Sometimes things aren't as bad as you'd imagined, and sometimes they are exactly the way you'd imagined them to be. I felt incredibly insecure, unsure of how I would ever keep up with all these geniuses. I was so shy in class that I rarely spoke up. I kept my awesomeness hidden under lock and key inside of me. I didn't want to risk letting it out, in fear that compared to others, I wasn't awesome at all.

I won't pretend that first year wasn't rough. Anytime you move someplace new or start a new job, it is going to take some adjustment to find your footing. Don't beat yourself up about it! We have all been there. But at some point, you're going to have to open that lock and unleash your awesomeness for the world to see. It *does* get better.

By sophomore year, I knew I had to push myself more. I had been accepted to Yale. I deserved to be there just as much as anyone else. And I slowly began to emerge from behind the guard I had put up: I spoke up in class and started to get involved in campus organizations.

Why are extracurricular activities so important? In high school, they're encouraged because they help us to become well-rounded, and more desirable to the colleges of our choice. But why do colleges even care about these activities? While you may be able to take tests and write papers with the best of them, academic learning is only one aspect of who you are. You can be incredibly confident in the classroom and completely insecure when you step out into the real world. Having confidence in both is key!

By the time I graduated, I had shed my shy-girl ways. But it didn't happen overnight. Instead, through a number of gradual steps, I began to put myself out there.

You have to start SMALL to go BIG.

My first small step was volunteering to be the website manager for the Asian American Students Association. Even though it was a minor role, participating in that group led to an opportunity to join the staff of the school newspaper and then, by junior year, to be promoted to publisher. By senior year, I was selected to be a part of the Yale Senior Class Council, composed of the top student leaders from across campus (athletes, musicians, newspaper staff, student government officers), who would be in charge of overseeing class events throughout the year.

As someone willing to put in the work, I ended up being the one to take charge of most of these events. And by year's end, both students and the administration ended up asking me, as a thank-you, to be the class's graduation chair. This involved planning Senior Week activities and the graduation ceremony; meeting with our graduation speaker, Tony Blair (who at the time was the prime minister of the United Kingdom); and giving an address at graduation itself.

And that is how I found myself onstage, in front of ten thousand people, giving a speech to my classmates about how we should stay focused on the good and optimistic about our futures, no matter what hardships we may face.

I was hesitant to give that speech; the shy girl who would never speak up in class still lived within me. But despite my hesitation, I knew I could face my fear and do it anyway. Every time I had faced something that I wasn't sure I could do, with enough practice and perseverance, I had stepped up to the moment, not wanting to live with regret.

As I took the stage, I took a breath and unleashed my awesomeness. I had spent hours preparing and had practiced enough to know, without a doubt, that I could do it.

As a fun surprise for my classmates, one of Yale's choirs joined me onstage in the middle of my speech. Together, we sang a college favorite, Bon Jovi's classic "Livin' on a Prayer."

The audience of ten thousand cheered.

Looking out from that stage, I stood there confident and capable, knowing how far I had come from the moment that I had first stepped on campus, afraid, insecure, and hiding. Here I was in front of everyone, not letting any fears hold me back.

ACCEPTING THE CHALLENGE

The kind of confidence I felt on that graduation stage—the kind that fills your chest with excitement and makes you feel on top of the world—is the key. I never would have built my own company without it. When I felt the seeds

YOUR BADASS GIRL
MOGUL READING LIST

Marian Wright Edelman, who founded the Children's Defense Fund and was the first African American woman admitted to the Mississippi Bar Association, famously said, "You can't be what you can't see." Below is a list of books about empowered, inspiring women and girls who break stereotypes and do the unexpected. They will allow you to see how much you are capable of.

***Ramona and Her Father* by Beverly Cleary.** I loved the Ramona books growing up, and especially this one about her relationship with her father when he loses his job. Even though she was just seven years old, Ramona dedicates herself to helping out her family. She knows she can contribute, and doesn't let her age slow her down.

***Eleanor Roosevelt: A Life of Discovery* by Russell Freedman.** I read this biography of Eleanor Roosevelt when I was in high school and was incredibly inspired by this bold, daring woman who aimed to accomplish more than people expected from a first lady. She redefined what that role was for the women who came after her.

***Hidden Figures: The American Dream and the Untold Story of the Black Women Mathematicians Who Helped Win the Space Race* by Margot Lee Shetterly.** This remarkable book tells the story of four African American women who were called to serve their country during the labor shortages of World War II, and who consequently were given the opportunity to work at NASA and highlight their mathematical skills. These women faced discrimination not just because of their race but also because of their gender. They were able to challenge the status quo, demand rights, and show that their brains were just as bright and their abilities just as extraordinary as those of the white men around them. Whether you read the book or watch the Oscar-nominated movie, this inspiring true story will encourage you to push boundaries and not let people limit you.

***Pride and Prejudice* by Jane Austen.** Elizabeth Bennet, the main character of this book, is an incredible example to me of a young woman who wasn't afraid to speak her mind, even in a society that didn't encourage it.

***Bossypants* by Tina Fey.** There is so much kindness and humor on every page of this book as comedian, author, and actress Tina Fey talks about what it was like to enter a field dominated by men and make a space for herself.

***Why Not Me?* by Mindy Kaling.** Mindy Kaling could easily be one of my best friends. So much of what she says in this book rings true to me, and I highly recommend it to anyone. It is not just a great read but also an empowering manifesto.

of Mogul growing, I would not have been able to see the opportunity and build it myself without confidence in my abilities. That doesn't mean it wasn't scary. It *was*! But I had learned by then to trust that I had what it takes. This trust came not only from responsibilities that I took on during college but also from pursuing jobs after graduation that I knew would develop the skill sets I needed to one day build my own company.

I first worked for two years at the investment bank Credit Suisse in its financial analyst program. I then attended Harvard Business School. After graduation, I accepted a job at CBS as a director of business development. I'll share throughout this book the decision-making process that led me to take on each of those jobs as well as many others that I did on the side. Each step was an essential confidence booster that allowed me to feel assured when the time came to build my own company that I had the skill set and ability to do what I dreamed of.

My conviction that it was time to create something on my own was born when I woke up one morning to learn that I had been named to *Forbes'* "30 Under 30." It was a surreal moment. At twenty-seven years old, I was one of the youngest directors at CBS. In the brief article that was under my picture, *Forbes* described my additional portfolio of work, from producing films, leading the Beijing International Screenwriting Competition, to co-authoring a business and technology book with my father and younger brother, David. (Yes, it was a busy time in my life, and I wasn't getting a ton of sleep, but I wouldn't change it for the world!)

As I opened my email, I had tons of messages from friends and family who had heard the news and were congratulating me. But I also had emails from people that I didn't know. Hundreds of them. From women and girls all over the world, who had seen the list, read about what I was doing, and wanted to hear how I had gotten these jobs in my twenties. They wondered how they could get these jobs, too.

I tried to carefully respond to each and every message I received. They varied in content and circumstance, but each girl was facing frustration, roadblocks, and what felt like limitations to how far she could rise in her respective society.

I didn't know exactly what to share, but I emailed each person back, writing of the strategies I used to reach out to people I admired, the places where I sought out opportunities, and the overall mentality that had driven me from the very beginning. Each time I pressed SEND, I was thankful for the opportunity to be a mentor.

And I couldn't help but remember the promise I had made to my grandmother and to myself when I was a teenager. I had focused on one day creating a company to empower women. My grandmother had been a pioneer, creating businesses and providing opportunities to others in need. I wanted to do the same.

And though I hadn't created a company yet, what I was doing each night was most definitely empowering

women. As weeks went by and I continued to get emails from new people each day, I also began to receive responses from those who had already reached out. Each was saying that my letter had changed her life. That she had gotten that interview, that job offer, that promotion she never thought would be possible.

It felt amazing to be connected to women around the world and to have the opportunity to encourage them and help them reach their goals. But I knew that answering emails every night until three in the morning was not sustainable. I knew that these women could likely offer one another support in ways that I was not even capable of. What if I could create a place where women could come together to share conversations—their questions, experiences, advice, and feedback? It could be a platform geared toward women and their goals—a living, breathing place where these women could support one another and where, at any given moment, you could see what was top-of-mind to women across the globe.

I had endless ideas about how this could take shape. There was only one problem.

I had no idea how to create it, and I didn't have the funds to hire a team of engineers.

My brother, David, had always been the tech prodigy in our family. But I hoped that if I could teach myself how to code, I could initially build this platform myself. I wanted to develop technical know-how and be able to understand every aspect myself. So I reached out to David and asked him how I could teach myself to code.

My ever-helpful brother, whom I proudly consider a mentor (even though I'm older!), pointed me to a couple of different resources and offered to step in whenever I might need him. For several months, after I got home from my job at CBS and finished work on my side projects, I would make myself a cup of tea, open my personal laptop, and teach myself Ruby on Rails, a coding language.

It wasn't easy. In fact, it took me an entire month to get through the first chapter of Michael Hartl's "Ruby on Rails Tutorial," which was literally just about what kind of software you needed to download on your computer.

But once I got through that chapter and finally started the nuts and bolts of creating a website, I loved getting to build something myself. I enjoyed what I was doing so much that, at twenty-seven, with no true plans in place, I resigned from CBS, taking the leap so I could focus on coding.

And before I knew it, I had a site up and running. It was far from perfect, and it would take months to continue tweaking it and improving it. But I was ready to put it out there and give the women who had written me access to one another. I could continue to improve the site in real time, if necessary. I sent the link to my parents and my brother to get some feedback and see how it would work for people outside. Then I knew it was time to release it to the world.

I had been collecting the emails of the women reaching out to me, a list that now numbered in the thousands. I sent the link to all of them, encouraging them to join the conversation online and have access not just to my thoughts and feedback but to those of other women across the globe. I knew that together we had the power to create a network of women supporting one another.

I clicked SEND and went to bed.

By the time I woke up the next morning, I realized that something viral was happening. David reached out to tell me that Mogul was getting a lot of traction. We watched in awe over the next few days as we reached 250,000 people. Then 500,000.

And by the beginning of that next week, nearly *one million* people.

I had no idea that the platform I had created would strike such a chord. Sure, I'd had big dreams for it. I knew it had vast potential. I knew, from the emails that I had received, that girls were looking for something like this.

But I hadn't expected that kind of growth, that Mogul could become one of the fastest-growing platforms for women worldwide.

I decided I needed to fully commit myself to this endeavor. I needed to work on Mogul all day, every day. Though I was young to run my own company, I knew how much I had learned during my time at Yale, Harvard Business School, Credit Suisse, CBS, and the many side jobs I'd had over the years. With every new task I had taken on, with every successful collaboration, it was another way for me to know how much I was capable of, to know what I had to offer the world. It was time to acknowledge the awesomeness within, and that I was ready to run this company.

TRUST THAT
YOU CAN

What confidence allows you to do is to step up to the plate and know that you have what it takes. Women notoriously don't apply for internships and jobs unless they are 100 percent qualified, whereas men apply for internships and jobs even if they are only 60 percent qualified. But it shouldn't be this way.

No matter who you are, don't allow the fact that you don't know something to hold you back. If you don't know how to do something, you can always learn. I taught myself to code so that I could build a technology company myself when I didn't have thc funds to hire engineers.

Take a page from Mindy and ask: *Why not me?* When an opportunity presents itself, to try out for the play, run for student governmcnt, or join a new club, say yes and trust that you can do it.

CONFIDENCE BOOSTERS

Having confidence and the knowledge that you are capable is the first step to realizing your dreams. You have to know that you have within yourself what it takes to succeed. And you do! It may not have been there from the day you were born, but take a moment and think about all the things you've done in your life. Whether it was crushing the SAT even though you hate taking tests, having your artwork chosen for a school exhibit, starting a new fundraiser for your school and watching the donations roll in, or running for student council and getting elected, each of your accomplishments is something to celebrate.

Think about how brave, strong, and smart you are. And now take all these amazing feelings and apply them to what you want to do next.

Every time you succeed at something, take a moment to acknowledge it. We are big on celebration at Mogul, so we have a "Weekly Wins" session every Friday, where everyone in the entire company takes turns sharing their greatest accomplishment for that week. It doesn't have to be something major, like signing a new client. It can be getting through your to-do list, or staying focused on a problem and finding a solution, or identifying a new way to collaborate with a different department. We do Weekly Wins because the shared wins produce passion and momentum for the week ahead. But we also do it because when you acknowledge and celebrate your own accomplishments, you set your sights that much higher the next time you go after something. You give yourself permission to aim high because you know how capable you are.

CREATE A "WEEKLY WINS" JOURNAL

Take a play from Mogul, and each Friday, review your week and write down five things that went well. If you have more than five, great—keep listing them! Recording your successes helps you exercise that confidence muscle. Don't just think about schoolwork; think about friendships and activities, and family life. Maybe you forgave a friend you'd been fighting with. Maybe you had a good conversation with your mom. Maybe you aced a tryout or made a new friend. Celebrate these moments! And then get ready for another incredible week to follow.

TIFFANY'S TOP TIPS FOR CONFIDENCE BUILDING

✓ **Learn a skill.** Identify a skill you've always wanted to acquire, and learn it. Take a lesson, enroll in a class, or reach out to a friend who already knows how. The more new skills you acquire, the more confidence you'll have.

✓ **Make something happen.** Whether it's asking someone you've had your eye on out on a date, trying out for the school play, or running for student government, take something that feels impossible and see if you can make it happen. Just try. Try your absolute best; give it your all. Obviously, you may get a no. That's *okay*. The experience gained will be helpful, regardless. Keep going, and don't give up. Try again, or try something comparable.

✓ **Echo a role model.** Do you have a role model that you look up to, who embodies something you want to be? Someone who inspires you, who keeps you focused on what is possible? Pick one thing you admire about her and then embody that positive quality as you follow in her footsteps. That commitment will keep you going even during the hard days ahead.

KRISTEN VISBAL
ARTIST AND CREATOR OF THE
FEARLESS GIRL STATUE

HOW TO BE FEARLESS

On November 30, 2016, I received a phone call from McCann New York, a worldwide advertising company. One of its clients, State Street Global Advisors of Boston, Massachusetts, wanted to create a statue of a little girl, in celebration of International Women's Day, and install this bronze figure three months later, on March 7, 2017. The plan was to place her, under the cloak of night and in the same manner, across from Wall Street's famous *Charging Bull* statue, located at Bowling Green in Lower Manhattan. Could I help?

With that, *Fearless Girl*, a more than fifty-inch (less than one-and-a-half meter) bronze statue of a little girl standing defiantly, with hands on hips,

KRISTEN VISBAL FACES THE *FEARLESS GIRL*.

was born. Little did we know what an overwhelming success the sculpture would become.

The intent of the statue is to highlight the role of women in the male-dominated financial community. She is a statement of the importance of women in business and a call to increase the number of women in decision-making roles. The child directly references the impact women will have on business tomorrow. Though *Charging Bull* remains a symbol of the strength of the American people and the bullish market, the placement of *Fearless Girl* sends the resounding message that the inclusion of women in business is imperative to the well-being of the global community.

State Street Global Advisors initiated a global conversation (in conjunction with the placement of *Fearless Girl*) on the importance of gender diversity in decision-making, specifically at the board level. The overwhelming research these gender diversity studies represent validates the importance of women in the workplace. Simultaneously, *Fearless Girl* has become synonymous with empowerment and courage, setting an example for women of all ages. She calls for valiant behavior in retaliation to gender stereotypes, which diminish and mask the invaluable resource women represent.

Fearless Girl is art at its very best, generating speculation and debate. Her placement started an important conversation about gender stereotypes and how these hinder productivity and enlightened decisions. *Fearless Girl* embodies the idea of true equality, an equality that will free the global community, creating a more productive and superior environment. Specifically, the sculpture represents support for women in leadership positions; the empowerment of young women; women's education; gender equality; the reduction of prejudice in the workplace through education; equal pay; and the general well-being of women. She is a figure to emulate.

Assuming the *Fearless Girl* position of power with chin lifted, feet firmly planted apart, and hands on hips, instills a quiet inner resolve and the determination to overcome. ⌣

CHAPTER TWO
FEELING YOUR BEST VERSUS LOOKING YOUR BEST

For most of my life, the women I saw on TV, in movies, and in magazines looked nothing like me. Let's face it—the popular conception of beauty in America (and especially in Texas, where I was growing up!) was blond hair and blue eyes. Even though our country has gotten more diverse, America's diversity hasn't always been represented in the media. For a good chunk of my life, I felt like an outsider and an ugly duckling.

It wasn't until I was an adult that I understood how messed-up these ideals are, and that by defining beauty and "normalcy" in such small terms, you leave 99 percent of the world out of the equation.

Being considered beautiful on the outside is never a goal I've striven to achieve, because I know that it's not what's on the outside that truly matters. I know, from examples in my own life and the world around me, that true beauty stems from the essence that exudes from inside. It's the emanation of your spirit and emotions.

Think about the following: You can be drop-dead gorgeous by societal and cultural standards, but if you are mean, judgmental, and unkind, those qualities make you ugly. Think of someone who may not be traditionally beautiful, but who exudes kindness, generosity, openness of spirit, and joy. They are beautiful in their own way. You feel beauty in their presence.

And just like beauty, confidence stems from inside. Confidence is about how you *feel*, not the package you present to the world. If you feel insecure, belittled, or unappreciated on the inside, no matter how you look on the outside, you won't be walking into a room with confidence. On the other hand, when you feel smart, happy, valued, and loved, you can walk into any room and command attention.

The journey to true self-confidence is not about trying to fit into the small box that society has deemed beautiful. It's about discovering what makes *you* feel your best, and comfortable in your own skin. Along the way, I've discovered small efforts that make a big impact on my ability to walk into a room with confidence. When *you* determine these "awaken your inner-badass" hacks, you'll discover your own shortcuts to feel like your very best self every single day. And when you feel your best, you do your best.

FIND A TRUE BEAUTY ICON

My parents loved classic American cinema and introduced my siblings and me to it very early on, when we were learning English. Sometimes I think my poised way of speaking today comes from watching those movies, with strong feminine characters portrayed by Marilyn Monroe and Audrey Hepburn. Audrey especially stood out to me, not just because of her poise on screen but because she was a natural beauty, never overly made-up, and she always looked comfortable in her own skin. It was clear she knew what looked best on her body, and she rarely veered from what worked for her, no matter what the current fashion trends.

She was true to herself and always focused on giving back.

Audrey grew up in the Netherlands during World War II, and, after the war, when much of the country was starving, she was one of many grateful recipients of essential nutrition and medical relief from the United Nations Children's Fund (UNICEF). When her Hollywood career ended and her children were raised, she dedicated the last five years of her life to UNICEF, traveling the world to provide aid to children who needed it. She visited war-ravaged countries so that she could share personally about the needs that remained and all that we in the US could do to help.

Audrey was kind and generous and devoted to others. Beautiful, both inside and out. She exemplified true beauty, and her beauty deepened as she aged. When you think of timeless beauty, it is beauty that stems from within.

Someone who ages gracefully has a shine in their eyes that is powerful and speaks of all the wisdom they have gathered within. It's about what's inside.

My other beauty idol was my mother. She had a similar poise about her. She had beautiful skin that she took great care of, and she always applied classic red lipstick before she left the house. I remember that as she raised my sister and me, she wanted to ensure that we took care of our skin and presented our natural beauty to the world. She never wanted me to wear much makeup on my face, to put on a mask, convinced that I didn't need it and that it would ruin my natural complexion. And after a few attempts at full-on foundation, I realized she was right! I would end up breaking out anytime I tried. To this day, I rarely wear foundation, preferring instead to have a clean face, just like my mother.

My mother is one of the most beautiful women I know because she carries herself with such grace and composure that she attracts attention. She is someone who does not speak loudly, but

Josh Castillon

FEELING LIKE A MOGUL.

speaks purposefully, and you feel like what she says will really matter. She doesn't fill up the room with chatter. She is careful with her words, but they are gems, precious, and worth their weight in gold.

She was always comfortable being who she was, in Paris and in Plano. She didn't try to conform to the culture she moved to, but had her own sense of style and her own kind of confidence. She was beautiful not only for her outer appearance but also for who she was not afraid to be.

We have examples of this all around us. Today, there are women challenging traditional American beauty standards, including models embracing their curves and natural body shape, who are stunningly beautiful not just for their features but because of the confidence that stems from every move they make. They show us how powerful it can be when you feel comfortable in your own skin. When you know what you bring to the table. When you aren't afraid to challenge the status quo and be something different.

My beauty idols are women who know who they are and how special they are. We are all born with inherent gifts that, when shared with the world, illuminate our inherent beauty. When we stop thinking about beauty as something that relates to our outer self, instead realizing that it stems from inside, we can recognize that we all have something to share, that beauty is not only the realm of supermodels but the realm of real, honest people. Your beauty could be your creativity, your ability to speak honestly and forthrightly with kindness, the way you can lighten the mood in a room with humor, how you bring out the best in your friends. *This* is what the world needs, not pretty packaging. So get in touch with your gifts, and then share them with the world.

OWNING YOUR UNIQUENESS

Before I could be truly comfortable in my own skin, I had to embrace the fact that I was often going to stand out in a room. Throughout my life, there has always been some characteristic that made me different from everyone else. In Paris, I was Asian. In Texas, I was

What are some of your best inner qualities?

How do you show them to the world?

What could you do to share them with your friends, family, school, or community?

Who is someone who you feel exudes beauty in their own way?

Asian with a French accent. In college in New England, I was Asian but now with a Texan twang. ("Y'all" really is more efficient to say than "you all.") Then in business school, I was among the youngest in my classes. Even when I entered the corporate world, I was often the youngest, the only Asian, or the only woman in the room.

I had to learn how to own my uniqueness and see it as a differentiator and a positive. Otherwise, I was always going to deal with impostor syndrome.

When I entered Harvard Business School, I knew I was going to be one of the youngest students in my class. It wasn't a surprise; it was something I was prepared for. I had wanted to go to business school since my senior year in college, with the hopes that it would help me further develop the right skill set for creating my own company. HBS was my dream, and I was shocked and thrilled when I received my acceptance during spring break that year. I ended up deferring my enrollment for two years so that I could work at Credit Suisse. But even with those two years of experience, I was just twenty-three when I entered business school, four years younger than the average first-year student.

Our class of nine hundred was split into ten different "sections," and these smaller groups of ninety students each would be the people we had classes with and thus became closest to. I was placed in what came to be called the "married section," since most of the students were already well-established in their careers and married with young kids, and this degree was their final step before they would be ready to start running companies.

The majority of the students in my section were white men—and then there was me: a twenty-three-year-old single woman, and a minority. And though I had gone to Yale, been publisher of the *Herald*, led our Senior Class Council, helped produce off-off-Broadway musicals, begun producing Hollywood movies, *and* worked at Credit Suisse, I felt small. Insignificant. Like I stood out, and not in a good way, but in a "who-let-*her*-in?" way.

There were many nights when I would have to give myself a pep talk just to head to class the next day. Class participation was a huge part of my grade, and I shied away from talking in class. I watched as my classmates confidently spoke up, sharing their opinions and adding to the discussion, regardless of whether they had anything new to truly add. I realized I could try to fade into the background because I didn't feel like I fit in, or I could speak up for the very reason that I would be able to share a different view. My perspective was necessary *because* it was different. It added something new and valuable to the conversation.

That shift allowed me to finally embrace that my uniqueness was actually a gift.

The fact is, as women, if we are going to be breaking down boundaries, we are often going to find ourselves the only woman in the room. We will look different, think different, and speak different from those who may surround us. That is *exactly* why we are needed.

Ultimately, I was the first HBS graduate to be honored on *Forbes'* "30 Under 30," and many classmates have since kindly described me as one of the most successful from our graduating class. I share all of this only to encourage you further if you sometimes feel like an underdog, as I did—to remind you that you cannot let your age or the fact that you are different hold you back. Many people think you have to have a lot of work experience under your belt before you can really get something out of business school. Or that there are certain boxes you need to check before you apply. I didn't follow a conventional path, but it was one that felt right to me. And it has led to Mogul's success today.

Currently, we are seeing more and more diversity on-screen, in the boardroom, and in government. But we still have a long way to go. Don't feel like you have to wait for someone who looks like you to lead the way. Former US Secretary of State Condoleezza Rice once said: "You can't wait for role models to look like you. If Sally Ride . . . had been waiting for a female

Audrey Froggatt

MOGULS COME FROM UNIQUE BACKGROUNDS AND DIVERSE PERSPECTIVES.

OWN YOUR UNIQUENESS: ROLE MODELS TO KEEP YOU FOCUSED

Take note of these amazing individuals who have taken the very thing that makes them unique and created something beautiful.

✓ **Madeline Stuart** (our Mogul Mentor for this chapter): Madeline is the world's first super-model with Down syndrome. After seeing a fashion show when she was just seventeen, she told her mom she wanted to model. And she has done just that, breaking down stereo-types about who should be represented on the runways, and proving that beauty comes from knowing your worth and not being afraid to go after what you want.

✓ **Lizzie Velasquez**: Born with an undiagnosed syndrome that prevents her from gaining weight, Lizzie has been the victim of extreme bullying, especially online, where she was once called "The Ugliest Woman in the World." But instead of hiding in shame, she has become an award-winning motivational speaker and author, helping others realize that they can stand up to abuse and that they can be beautiful in their own way.

✓ **Ashley Graham**: As one of America's most famous plus-size models, Ashley has graced the covers of *Vogue*, *Glamour*, *Elle*, and more, and is the first plus-size model to be featured on the cover of the *Sports Illustrated* swimsuit issue, as well as to get a major cosmetics contract. Her daily mantra?

I am bold.
I am brilliant.
I am beautiful.

astronaut role model, she would have never done it!"

Own your uniqueness and allow it to *give* you confidence, not deplete it.

REDEFINING THE STANDARD

When I started Mogul, I wanted to create a company that could battle the barriers that women face when they try to enter spheres where they haven't been welcomed. One of the goals of Mogul is to help transform our society from one that tries to put us in boxes where we are to be admired for our beauty instead of our brains. In particular, we have learned to focus on advertising. According to the World Economic Forum, women are depicted as intelligent in only 2 percent of advertising, even though in the United States, we are now more likely to have bachelor's degrees than our male counterparts.

Think about a few of the ad campaigns you might have skipped past on your way to viewing another episode of *The Walking Dead*. If there was a woman in the commercial, she was likely (1) doing some kind of domestic work, (2) getting her hair done, (3) looking at herself in the mirror, or (4) the object of a guy's attention. And then, of course, there are the print ads in fashion magazines that make it seem like we should all be size 0, putting on a full face of makeup, half-clothed, to go out on the town.

Mogul was created so that we could address this stereotyping and change the conversation.

One of our divisions at Mogul, Mogul Studios, works with Fortune 1000 companies on such advertising campaigns. From the very start, we held these companies to certain standards when it came to how they portrayed women in their ads. If we saw a woman portrayed in a stereotypical light, we tried to open their eyes to other options. Why is she in the kitchen? Could she instead be in the boardroom? Why is she wearing a miniskirt? These companies had hired us to help them connect with the Mogul audience. This guidance was one way we could do just that.

But in 2017, we decided to take it a step further. At a United Nations gathering of Fortune 1000 chief marketing officers, UN representatives, and reporters, I asked everyone to stand up and commit to what we call "The Mogul Standard." They repeated the following pledge out loud:

"I pledge to ensure that all marketing and advertising produced by my company will present women in a positive and diverse light in terms of race, physicality, and context, and avoid stereotyping. We stand by efforts to drive positive social change and to reshape the standards that are presented to young girls and women with respect to perceptions of beauty and gender roles."

As soon as they finished reciting, the UN chamber erupted in a standing ovation.

I cannot wait to see the effect this pledge might have on the kinds of images this and future generations of girls are presented with as they are growing up. It will take time, and we will still be presented with unrealistic portrayals of beauty. When you are faced with an image that implies you should focus only on your outer appearance—that therein lies your value—turn off the TV, flip the page, or change the channel. Know that it is not true. Who you are is so much more than what people see on the outside.

DRESS FOR *YOU*

I'm not going to lie and say that how you present yourself doesn't matter. It's not like you see me wearing sweatpants and a ponytail in every picture (though if you'd had a camera during those early days building Mogul, that's exactly what you would have found!). Especially when you are the public face of your company or brand, your image does matter, and I've learned that when I feel like I look my best, I'll act my best. But again, how I *feel* is what is important, not what others think. I have two beauty products that I consistently use to allow myself to quickly feel pulled-together: red

MY THREE FAVORITE FEMALE EMPOWERMENT AD CAMPAIGNS

#FearlessGirl: The little girl that stands opposite *Charging Bull* in Manhattan was conceptualized by an advertising company in celebration of International Women's Day. You can read about her creation in our Mogul Mentor section in Chapter One. *Fearless Girl* is an example for all of us: She is determined, she knows her worth, and she isn't going to back down.

#LikeAGirl: For a 2015 Super Bowl ad, Always created an ad campaign that took the phrase *like a girl*, which is often used in a derogatory way (i.e., he throws "like a girl") and turned it on its head, letting little girls redefine what "like a girl" really was. The ad pointed out that it isn't until puberty that girls start to feel insecure about their abilities. When the ad producers asked younger girls what "like a girl"

.meant, the phrase meant doing the best that they could. It was an amazing, empowering, and revolutionary ad, and it has continued to be relevant in our culture today.

#IAmAMogul: We created the #IAmAMogul campaign to encourage women everywhere to identify themselves as moguls. We started with our Mogul Influencers, but the campaign extended broadly, with women across the world claiming that they have power, influence, and a chance to change the world. Now it's your turn:

#IAmAMogul because: _____

_____

_____

_____

_____

_____

_____

MOGULS COME IN ALL BEAUTIFUL SHAPES AND SIZES.

lipstick, because it helps me stand out even when I'm not the loudest in the room, and black eyeliner (typically a cat eye), because it makes my eyes stand out with sharpness. When I have those two components in place, I feel confident and beautiful, no matter what. I feel ready for whatever may come.

Your routines will change as you go through different phases of life and discover new things about yourself.

Your style may change or your job may require a different dress code. But if you remember to stay focused on what feels best to you, staying authentic to your personal style and your comfort, you'll always broadcast the kind of confidence that makes people take notice. You'll increase your ability to command a room, feel confident in every moment, and know that you're powerful enough to handle what is to come.

DETERMINE YOUR CONFIDENCE HACKS

When do you feel like your best self?

- What are you doing?

- What are you wearing?

- How does it make you feel?

How could you incorporate these elements into your everyday life so that you always feel great? It could be something as simple as identifying what kind of fabric makes you feel comfortable but confident. It could be listening to a certain song before you go into soccer practice or a test. It could be developing a mantra that you say each morning before you start your day—like *I'm doing great. I have so much to be thankful for. So now how can I help others?* These small things can have big impact on your overall feelings.

How you look should be an extension of who you are on the inside. You can be someone who loves fashion and expressing your individuality through what you wear. You can be someone, like me, who pretty much wears the same thing every day. It doesn't matter what you wear as long as it works for you, allows you to get in touch with the gifts inside yourself, and gives you the confidence to share these gifts with the world.

mogul mentor
MADELINE STUART
THE WORLD'S FIRST SUPERMODEL
WITH DOWN SYNDROME

Just like every girl, I have dreams. My dream was born the day I saw a fashion show with my mom when I was seventeen years old. From that moment on, I knew I wanted to be a model. But I knew I had some work to do. I needed to change society's perception of the word *beauty*.

I was born with Down syndrome and thus don't fit the mold for a typical model. But though I knew there would be plenty of people who took one look at me and said, "No, you can't," I said, "Yes, I can," and didn't let being different stop me. I knew there were countless girls who felt completely left out of the fashion industry because of the ridiculous standard that had been set. If I could break down those boundaries, I could help other girls feel like they, too, didn't need to worry about being different. That they, too, could

MADELINE STUART

© Wildflower Portaits

celebrate their differentness.

Turning my dream into a reality wasn't easy. But I worked hard to get myself into the best shape possible, and then took some stunning photographs.

When I posted them on social media, they went viral and caught the attention of the very people I'd hoped to reach—the fashion industry.

Today, my dream has become a reality.

I've walked the runways of New York Fashion Week for the past five seasons, along with Paris Fashion Week, London Fashion Week, LA Fashion Week, Mercedes-Benz China Fashion Week, to name a few; I've been named "Model of the Year" by Melange; I was the first person with Down syndrome to be the face of a cosmetics company, GlossiGirl; and I am the only person in history with an intellectual disability to get a working visa in the US.

I am proud to say that I am the first professional model with Down syndrome who defied all societal odds of what *beauty* used to mean, and made progress to reshape what the definition of that word really is in the modern world.

I want my story to be one that shows girls across the world—no matter where they are from, what they look like, or what cards they have been dealt in life—that they can overcome obstacles to fulfill their dreams, too. If someone tells you no, make the choice to keep going, and you will find a yes elsewhere.

It is through our own naïveté that we discriminate against people who are different. But the more of us who step up and out of the shadows, the more opportunities we give others to realize how wide the spectrum of beauty can be.

True beauty is the spirit that lives inside each one of us. ♛

CHAPTER THREE
SCHEDULING YOUR WAY TO SUCCESS (AND LESS STRESS)

You may think that to build your own company, you've got to work around the clock, with no time for fun. But here's a mantra of mine:

You can't be your BEST when you're stressed.

To be a Girl Mogul, you've got to find balance and make sure that you are taking care of yourself along the way. If you do, you don't have to worry about becoming burned out by the time you are twenty. In fact, I'll show you that if you find your passions and make them your work, you are actually re-energized by work instead of depleted. And that's the key. Stress and anxiety drain your energy and hinder your progress. It's okay to feel them, and you will at times, but that's when you know to implement your tools to overcome them. In this chapter, I present the tricks I've used to stay focused, healthy, happy, and ultimately, ready to keep striving toward my goals. Using these strategies will keep you from burning out so that each day you'll wake up inspired to start again.

LET IT GO

When I was growing up, my father would drive us to our various after-school activities in our red Nissan minivan. And he always played audiotapes narrated by a man named Dale Carnegie, a pioneer in the field of self-help, whose books, like *How to Stop Worrying and Start Living,* have sold millions of copies. People have been using Dale's books and tapes for years, to become stronger salespeople, better leaders, less stressed, and more empowered.

Wisdom and inspiration can come from unexpected places, and as a young girl gazing absentmindedly out onto the streets of Plano from the back of our minivan, I was especially inspired by his philosophies, as they seemed to have come from years that he had spent in a noble and faraway land (the Midwest). Even though I didn't realize it at the time, I was learning resilience, positive thinking, and self-improvement as we carpooled from activity to activity.

I know understanding these concepts early on laid the groundwork for me becoming the Girl Mogul I am today.

I'm sure I don't have to tell you, but the world sometimes seems like an anxiety-creation machine. Whether it is the news, studying for a big test, worrying about how you'll get into the college of your dreams, finding an after-school job, or even agonizing about a relationship, there are an infinite number of potential stressors of all kinds in every single day.

But there is a trick that Dale Carnegie taught me. When you get caught up in the moment and find yourself worrying about whatever problem you are facing, take a moment and ponder one question: Is this one moment, in which you're feeling stressed or irritable, so important that it could impact your life five years from now?

And most often, the answer is no.

You didn't get invited to a party. Will this matter in five years? No.

You are running late to an activity. Will this matter in five years? No way.

You're fighting with a frenemy. Will this matter in five years? Nope.

You forgot about a quiz and received a low grade. Will this matter in five years? I think you know the answer by now.

That's not to say that you can't be disappointed by these situations. You can. But you can also recognize that your entire life isn't derailed. There will be another party. There will be other pop quizzes. You can remember to plan more time to get to that next activity.

So, when the moments of today start to weigh you down, turn your focus to the big picture. If you do that, the smaller disappointments aren't as consequential.

Now that doesn't mean you should shirk responsibility or blow off your tests. I'm just saying that you need to do your best, and then trust that your best is good enough. There is no amount of worrying that will make the results any different. You'll just stress yourself out and then not be able to perform at your peak.

Everyone faces stress. It is about how you deal with it. Do you invite it in to wreak havoc on your life? Or can you take a deep breath and let it go? Let the moment pass and move on into your future.

MY STRESS-FREE SECRET

Find yourself stressing out about grades, friends, or gossip?

Write down something that is really stressing you out right now:

Then take a moment and ask yourself: *Will I remember this in five years? Will this truly matter 1,826 days down the road?*

MAKING DECISIONS

There are many times in life when you will be in an uncomfortable limbo, when you need to make a decision and there is something to be lost and gained with each option. Your decision-making skills during such moments are crucial to success in life. If you struggle with how to move through the emotion and the upset that you experience at these points, then remember to take a deep breath, clear your head, think through the options, and make the best decision you can. Maybe you are someone who needs to write a pros-and-cons list for each option. Maybe you need to talk it through with a trusted friend, and through the conversation, the answer will become clear. Figure out what process works for you and stick with it when you face important decisions. It is such a valuable skill to develop, and will serve you well through your lifetime. If you're really on the fence, and no process is working to help you decide, trust your instincts. You'll be surprised how much you already know when you listen to your inner voice.

Here's an example from my high school years.

When I was first applying to colleges, I really thought I wanted to go to Stanford. So when I got my acceptance letter, I was thrilled. I couldn't believe it and began envisioning my life in sunny Silicon Valley. But I hadn't visited any colleges before applying. I didn't want to waste my parents' hard-earned money visiting a place that I didn't think I would really get into.

Yet I knew I should visit Stanford before I actually enrolled. And admitted-students weekend there was the same weekend as my senior prom.

Now, prom was something I had envisioned myself going to from the moment we moved to America. It is one of those classic American high school moments conveyed in countless movies I had watched over the years. *Pretty in Pink. 10 Things I Hate About You. She's All That. Footloose.*

I had to choose: visiting Stanford or going to prom.

Looking back, I think I used Dale Carnegie's trick. *Five years from now, will I regret not going to prom? Maybe. Five years from now, will I regret not making sure that I went to the right college? Yep.* I knew that I would regret it if I didn't ensure that Stanford was the right place for me.

I was definitely bummed to think

I would be missing this wonderful tradition that our class had been looking forward to for years. But I took a deep breath and let go of the stress. I focused on the future and the trip I now had planned. I also made the best of the situation by helping my friends pick out dresses and cheering them on as they found their respective dates. To me, that was the best of both worlds.

Audrey Froggatt

WORK HARD TO BE CHILL

My friends and family have always said that I am "the chillest hardworking person" they know. That mentality was not only part of what I learned from Dale Carnegie but also arose from being superdisciplined with my time. One of my no-fail strategies for dealing with stress is being hyperprepared. When you are prepared, you don't need to stress, because you know you put in the time to be ready for what may come next.

I'm the opposite of a procrastinator. When I know I have an assignment due, I schedule specific times to work on that assignment so that I can be sure it is complete by the deadline. In high school, I was so precise I would schedule out each hour. On Mondays, I knew I had lacrosse until 5 P.M. From 5 to 6 P.M., I would work on math. From 6 to 7 P.M., I'd work on my history assignment. The hour from 7 to 8 P.M. was always reserved for a family dinner, where we would set aside distractions and enjoy delicious homemade

Vietnamese dishes while connecting as a family. Then it was back to work. From 8 to 10 P.M., I would read several chapters of the book I needed to finish for English class by the end of the week, in the exact increments that would enable me to evenly space out my progress.

I would often have a schedule like this for the entire week, so that I knew I could complete every assignment on time.

I know this kind of hour-by-hour scheduling can sound a bit intimidating, and like you're giving yourself even more work. But, trust me, it really can save you a lot of time, allowing you more time for relaxation, and it eases stress, because you have a plan to stick to. My weekends rarely had to be filled with assignments, but instead would be filled with plenty of time with friends, and also weekly trips to the movie theater with my family.

I took this scheduling tactic with me to college and business school, and it has served me well in every area of my life ever since. When I worked at CBS, I was also doing several projects on the side, so I would schedule my after-work hours this way. Here's an example:

- Leave the office around 6 P.M. and head to a dinner, either with a business associate, a collaborator, a friend, or my boyfriend at the time.

- Head home and catch up on email from 8 to 10 P.M.

- Work on producing films from 10 P.M. to 12 A.M.

- Work on the launch of a new initiative, the Beijing International Screenwriting Competition, from 12 to 2 A.M.

I know it sounds intense, but by giving myself these periods of focus, I was able to accomplish a lot in a short amount of time. I had several goals that were important to me, and it was worth the time to make them happen. Not every season of my life was this packed-in. But I know that ultimately, this kind of scheduling is what allowed me to learn to code in the wee hours, leading to the creation of Mogul.

STAY PRESENT
TO STAY CALM

To keep myself from stressing on even the busiest of days, I try to stay in the moment, instead of thinking of what I just did or where I am going. Stress comes from worrying about something that you already did or how something in the future is going to go. When you stay focused just on the now, you let all that worry fade away. And when that moment is over, you move on to what is next.

If you are meeting with someone, for example, try to stay truly engaged with what they are saying, responding emotionally and maintaining eye contact. Keep your phone put away. Everyone has something they know better than someone else; over the course of your meeting, try to figure out what that piece of knowledge is so you can learn. Your curiosity and attention will genuinely make the other person feel at ease, making you further at ease as well, and you'll be rewarded with a more worthwhile conversation and a more solid bond.

This habit has personally allowed me to forge a deeper relationship with whomever I'm meeting. One of my high school teachers mentioned that she'd once met a former US president, and he'd made her feel like she was the only person in the room. He was completely focused on her and that moment, and she truly felt his presence. I've striven to be that way ever since. If you are fully present in the moment, you can make someone feel truly significant and respected, and that is the foundation of a strong relationship.

PACE YOUR SCHEDULE SO YOU CAN REMAIN CALM AT ALL TIMES.

BUILD YOUR STRESS-FREE SCHEDULE

My schedule is superpacked these days, with back-to-back meetings followed by speaking engagements and travel. And while every night I review my schedule for the next day in order to mentally prepare for each moment and visualize what success might look like for each meeting, once the day begins I stay focused in the present. I can't be thinking about the next meeting, or it will derail the one I'm in. I stay fully in the moment and take the day one moment, one meeting, one interaction at a time. This allows me to stay calm, focused, and dialed-in, all day long.

Here's how to build a schedule to help you map out your week and enable you to feel hyperprepared for each moment, leaving you little need to stress. I'm using homework assignments as examples, but it can be used for any task.

First, write out all of the short-term assignments you have that need to be completed within one or two days. Plan to complete them the night before they are due. In other words, if a piece of homework is due on Wednesday morning, make sure to prioritize it for Monday or Tuesday evening. Then make a list of the long-term projects you have that will require more time to complete—for example, a research paper. Break it down into milestones, with smaller goals that build to the final one. If you figure out a way to make incremental daily progress on these long-term projects, you can easily finish in advance of the deadline. For example, if the research paper is due on Friday and must be twelve pages, try to block out 5 to 7 P.M. from Monday to Wednesday in order to write four pages each day. That means you'll have completed the paper by Wednesday evening, leaving you plenty of buffer time to check over the paper on Thursday. Scheduling the same block of time each day to carry out this incremental daily progress isn't necessary, but it does generally help your body and

mind to quickly recognize your established routine and thus aid your overall efficiency and productivity.

Practice making a schedule with the following worksheet. You can make copies to print out and fill in each week.

I stay fully in the moment.

schedule

Short-Term Projects

_____

_____

_____

_____

_____

_____

_____

Long-Term Projects

_____

_____

_____

_____

_____

_____

_____

Monday

8 A.M.–3 P.M. _____

4 P.M. _____

5 P.M. _____

6 P.M. _____

7 P.M. _____

8 P.M. _____

9 P.M. _____

10 P.M. _____

Tuesday

8 A.M.–3 P.M. _____

4 P.M. _____

5 P.M. _____

6 P.M. _____

7 P.M. _____

8 P.M. _____

9 P.M. _____

10 P.M. _____

Wednesday

8 A.M.–3 P.M. _____

4 P.M. _____

5 P.M. _____

6 P.M. _____

7 P.M. _____

8 P.M. _____

9 P.M. _____

10 P.M. _____

Friday

8 A.M.–3 P.M. _____

4 P.M. _____

5 P.M. _____

6 P.M. _____

7 P.M. _____

8 P.M. _____

9 P.M. _____

10 P.M. _____

Thursday

8 A.M.–3 P.M. _____

4 P.M. _____

5 P.M. _____

6 P.M. _____

7 P.M. _____

8 P.M. _____

9 P.M. _____

10 P.M. _____

break it down into milestones.

THE BEST VERSION OF YOURSELF

There will always be times when you find yourself slipping into patterns that aren't the best for you—when you don't make time for self-care, and your body and mind feel the consequences.

After I resigned from CBS and started Mogul, I started down a four-month path where I hardly left my apartment. Mogul was exploding so fast, and I was a one-person team. I leaned on David when the site would crash, given the rocket-ship growth, but everything else was on my plate: interacting with users, moderating new content, designing graphics, pitching investors, and finalizing partners. So I worked from eight in the morning until three or four the next morning, leaving my room only to go to the bathroom and grab a few bites to eat. I wasn't nourishing myself at all.

Then, about a year after its creation, when we were running Mogul with a staff of four, we secured an office space

a block from my apartment in a building called The Yard. And next door to The Yard was a delicious Chinese restaurant. We began to order in Chinese food every day, and I wish I could say that I ordered veggies and chicken for each meal. Instead, I was drawn to the more flavorful choices, drenched in chili oil. That delicious yet far from healthy diet, combined with the fact that I pretty much sat at my desk all day, only walking the one hundred steps to my apartment to fall into bed and then do it all over again, was not a formula for health and wellness.

I've always been an active person. I'm someone who needs to move every day to feel my best. In high school, I did Taekwondo and lacrosse, and even if I didn't officially "exercise" during the day, I would turn on music first thing in the morning and dance around as I was brushing my teeth. In college, I took a modern dance class. When I worked in investment banking at Credit Suisse, with notoriously long hours, I made sure to schedule an hour or two per day to do Pilates. When I was at

CBS, I'd go for a run in the mornings before walking to the office through Central Park.

But when Mogul was starting up, I was like a new mom, tending to her baby's every need. I felt like Mogul needed me to be focused on it every single moment. If there was a choice between getting more sleep or exercise, and working on Mogul, I always chose Mogul.

Soon, I felt lethargic and far from the best version of myself.

This was when Mogul was first receiving a lot of press attention, so there are countless pictures and videos of me during this time. And I look tired, puffy, and dulled-down in those photos. Like my inner light wasn't able to shine, even though I was successful, because I wasn't taking care of myself. It was time to prioritize myself again and find a way to schedule exercise into my daily routine, so that I could get back to feeling my best.

I had to find an exercise that I truly loved, that I would look forward to doing each morning. I soon realized that dance classes were something I really enjoyed. I could often do them with a friend, which allowed us to spend time bonding while also doing something healthy for our bodies. Today, I go to a dance studio in New York City every morning at 7 A.M. It's on my schedule, no matter what. Unless I'm traveling, I'm there every morning.

I also began using an app called MyFitnessPal, which enabled me to see what I was actually eating each day, and I realized I was making a lot of unhealthy choices. What you put in your body greatly affects your energy level, and it can make you feel energized or like you want to take a nap. Using an app like this one really helped me to improve the choices I was making each day. On a day when I was thinking about eating a candy bar, I would go to put that information in the app and realize that it wasn't a nourishing choice. Did I want to eat that one candy bar that might taste good in the moment but leave me hungry in an hour? Or did I want to eat a delicious and filling meal (often the same number of calories!), which would leave me satisfied for the rest of the day? Using the app has allowed me to make better choices, which has led to feeling stronger, clearer, and like the best version of myself.

So make sure that in your day-to-day life you are finding ways to take care of yourself. Determine what kind of movement you actually enjoy. Not everyone loves running or taking classes! Maybe you enjoy biking and can start to bike to school. Maybe you love yoga and can incorporate it into your afternoon schedule to de-stress after a busy school day. Find ways to make exercise a part of your life.

Food is also an essential part of our day, and we face choices three times a day (at least!). Your body will crave and require different things than mine, but stay focused on how your meals are nourishing you and providing fuel for your activities to come. Although I know our culture likes to focus on good and bad foods, just think about what your body truly needs. That focus will usually guide you in the right direction.

MAKE YOUR SCHEDULE WORK FOR YOU

Today my days are busier than ever as Mogul continues to grow at a rapid pace across the globe. I've found that when life gets busy, I need to stay structured and have routines that will set me up for success.

Below are some things that I do every day to make sure I'm taking care of myself. As you read what works for me, I invite you to stop being reactive to your days and instead be proactive about what you need to feel your best and keep stress at bay.

Don't hit snooze. I usually wake up with the sun and rarely set an alarm. But if you do need that wake-up call, don't hit snooze! The extra five minutes of sleep will not make you feel more rested and, in fact, will likely make you feel drowsier. Try to get up as soon as the alarm goes off, ready to start your day. Maybe have your alarm be a song that makes you happy and energized, so that you can dance your way out of bed

TIFFANY'S FAVORITE
SONGS TO GET
YOUR ENERGY UP

"Teenage Dream" by Katy Perry

One of my best friends, Stephanie, and I love this song. It is light, fun, and energizing. We dance to it together all of the time (and even did at her wedding!).

"Club Can't Handle Me" by Flo Rida

This song reminds me of my business school days. It has a great beat, plus it makes me remember this very special time in my life. Also, we actually celebrated Mogul's first anniversary on a yacht with Flo Rida, and he performed this song. It was brilliant!

"Feel So Close" by Calvin Harris

When I was living in New York City right after college graduation, this was one of my favorite songs to get ready to each morning.

"Die Young" by Kesha

Kesha represents such strength and courage, and her music is unabashedly honest and inspiring. This song reminds me of my years of hustling and bustling in New York, before I started Mogul.

"Sorry Not Sorry" by Demi Lovato

We dance to this song every morning at the dance studio. There is something about the catchy melody but also the message of female empowerment that always awakens my body and spirit.

and to the bathroom. Keep the music on as you get ready and move your body. This helps wake you up and gets your endorphins flowing.

move your body

Exercise. If you can, try to exercise first thing in the morning. That way, you can cross it off your mental to-do list and you won't be able to cancel it later when other things inevitably come up that demand your attention. It doesn't need to be a full exercise class. It could be a quick run around your neighborhood, a yoga class through an app on your phone, a quick set of exercises in your room. If you have limited mobility, it could be some breathing or mindfulness exercises to get your blood flowing and your mind in a positive space. The point is, you are taking time to focus on yourself right from the start.

Dress to kill. I always choose what I'm going to wear the night before so I'm not faced with indecision first thing in the morning. I also have a standard outfit that I wear, almost a uniform, to cut down on decision-making and ensure that I'm always wearing something that I feel comfortable in. My uniform is usually a black dress and white pearl earrings. In my current profession, and with my days being packed full of various activities, I know that a black dress and pearls are always appropriate. Even people in fashion use the "uniform" trick! Think of Jenna Lyons, former president of J.Crew and her funky eyeglasses, straight-legged trousers, and preppy blazer. Or Anna Wintour, with her tailored dresses and skirts, and signature sunglasses.

dress to kill

Obviously, if you like to vary your wardrobe, this tip isn't for you, but it does cut down on decision-making in the morning! If you are required to wear an actual uniform to school, find an accessory that makes you feel like you stand out or are able to express your individuality. Never underestimate the power of accessories. If I'm going to be on my feet a lot that day, I tend to wear flats. If I have a fancy event in the evening, I'll pack heels in my bag to change into. And my go-to accessory is always red lips!

Eat three healthy meals a day. I make sure that I have eating time scheduled into my day because I know I cannot perform at my best if I am hungry. I often bring food into every meeting I organize, to make it more social and fun, and to keep us fueled. And I love to combine professional with personal by inviting associates to dinner and lunch, so that we can eat while also getting to know one another and discovering new ways to collaborate.

The night before, visualize. Every night when I look over my calendar for the next day, I take a moment to visualize how I want each event or meeting to go. What are my hopes and goals? What would it look like if the best outcome actually happened? Then I make a mental note to stay focused on that outcome during my day. Sometimes I even jot these goals in the margins of my calendar, so I can be easily reminded. You can do the same for school, envisioning what success would be like in each class.

envision success

Sleep! Okay, you've probably already noticed that I don't get a lot of sleep. So when it is time to sleep, I am very serious about it. I make sure the room is dark and my phone is in do-not-disturb mode. And when you are still growing, as you likely still are, you need sleep and as much of it as you can get! Sleep helps your brain develop, allows you to approach the next day refreshed and ready for what's to come, and will keep you from getting sick. I know school starts *early*, even if you aren't an early bird. So try to limit the distractions you face at night that might prevent you from going to bed when you are supposed to. Set an alarm for bedtime and stick to it. Make sure to shut down social media thirty minutes or more beforehand, to ensure that you don't get sucked in and because the blue light from your screen can inhibit sleep. Then pick up a book or listen to some relaxing music, and get ready to drift into blissful sleep.

These routines and structures are the anchors of your day. Every day looks very different, but these anchors will keep you tuned in to yourself and what your body needs so that you can truly be performing at your peak.

DRESS TO WIN

What are the clothes that you feel really good in? List the items that make you feel really confident, and decide from there what could become a "uniform" or another go-to outfit:

1. _____

2. _____

3. _____

4. _____

5. _____

6. _____

7. _____

8. _____

9. _____

10. _____

TOP TRICKS
FOR TUNING BACK
IN TO YOU

Take a bath. When things get crazy and I feel stress starting to nip at my heels, I take time for a luxurious bath. Get one of those amazing bath bombs and soak your body while you allow yourself to breathe deep and relax. If you don't have much time, even a brief shower will do. Sometimes, during that mental break, just listening to the sound of water hitting the bathtub, I find that solutions to problems I've been facing will suddenly reveal themselves. When you relax, your brain can do its best work, too.

Do something that you love. Whether it is going to the movies, curling up with or listening to a good book, playing the guitar, painting, or hiking, do something that brings you joy.

Do something for someone else. Sometimes just taking the focus off yourself allows you to realize how blessed you truly are. So pick some flowers for your mom or go to the store and pick out your best friend's favorite candy. Even taking the dog for a walk or running an errand for a neighbor can ultimately cheer you up as well.

Change your surroundings. If you can, go outside; fresh air gives you endorphins. Look for a green space, with trees and green grass. Being in nature can provide a grounding for you and help you feel connected to the world around you. But even if you just go into the next room, changing up the scene will give your brain a break.

Get together with your friends. Friends are the best medicine if you are feeling down or uninspired. They will make you laugh, they will remind you who you are, and they will provide both counsel and encouragement if you need it.

TINA EXARHOS

CHIEF CONTENT OFFICER OF NOWTHIS AND FORMER CHIEF MARKETING OFFICER OF MTV

No matter where you are in life right now, you'll one day decide to get a job. Your reasons for getting that job will probably be motivated by a number of different factors—you need money for college, or you're saving for a special camp. I got my first job while I was in high school so I could buy concert tickets. That was all the motivation I needed. When I got to college, I had two jobs: one, an unpaid internship in the media business; and another, a paid retail position. My passion continued to be music, and I worked while my friends were partying, just so I could go see shows.

Making money was always a means to an end for me . . . until I realized I could get paid to do what I loved. Once I started pursuing a career that gave me so much personal satisfaction, it didn't strike me for a long time that I was adding as much value to the company's

TIFFANY PHAM AND TINA EXARHOS

bottom line as it was adding to my personal growth. In any job, the work has to be mutually beneficial. When you realize that, the relationship you have with work changes in the best possible way.

I always loved working, and was lucky to have entered into a fulfilling career at a very young age, but I never imagined I could or would make real money. There was always a voice in the back of my head that told me I could never make more than I was making at any given moment in time, or that I didn't deserve to make more, or that I was lucky that I was even getting paid! Those voices made me superconservative about how I spent money and invested, and I didn't stretch myself at all. I wish someone had told me that I had the potential to earn big! I wish someone had told me to gamble when you're young—to bet on yourself. To know your worth and assume that you will keep rising up.

I've had an incredibly rewarding career, and absolutely love what I do. When I think about it, my entire career trajectory has been driven by the following questions, which I've asked myself over and over again through the years:

Am I learning?

Am I growing?

Does the work I'm doing have meaning and purpose?

Do I respect and admire the people I work with and for?

I spent so many years at the same company not because I was afraid of trying something new, but because my opportunities were expansive. I kept learning, and I kept growing. And I loved it.

Don't let others tell you what your career path should look like. When you are thinking about a new opportunity, whether it's a part-time job or which college to attend, make sure you are clear about what is driving your decision-making process. Focus on opportunity, not ego. So often, we get frustrated if someone else gets a more prestigious opportunity or a bigger job title. Don't worry about other people. We need to look out for ourselves, and to make sure we're getting credit for the work we do each day. But don't make decisions based only on title and salary. Those are important factors but not the only things that lead to a fulfilling career. Do you love what you are doing? Are there opportunities for growth and expansion? If your boss won't offer a raise, can you ask for more responsibility? **Chart your own path to finding meaningful work and getting what you feel you truly deserve. Always be learning.** ♛

CHAPTER FOUR
FAILING FORWARD

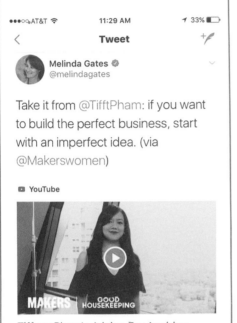

our family made during my childhood, I was forced out of my comfort zone, and while I didn't always feel immediately at ease, my ability to adjust, learn, and grow through the discomfort was a lesson in resilience. Life is not a series of perfect moments. There are ups and downs and in-betweens. It may not look like you are succeeding every single moment. But if you keep focused on the future, you'll learn something essential. You'll learn the art of failing forward.

FAILURE IS NOT A BAD WORD

Embracing failure is a popular concept in the startup world. In fact, many serial entrepreneurs love to discuss their failures just as much as their successes! Why? Because these failures are often what eventually led to success. The lessons learned and the mistakes made were all ultimately leading to that big win.

My parents raised me according to this guiding principle: Things will get hard, transitions are a necessary part of life, but you have to take chances to get where you want. I know this attitude was yet one more thing that allowed me to be the mogul I am today. With every move

I grew up far from the Silicon Valley culture, but my father instilled these same lessons in me from the beginning. He was always focused on learning and taking what he could from every experience, good or bad. When my parents immigrated, first to France from Vietnam, and then to Texas, they never let the culture shock get to them. Instead, they were open, curious, and excited about each new adventure that life brought them. I'm sure they must have felt like they were starting over at times, but I never saw them discouraged. My parents taught me that as long as you are learning something new, you are moving forward, and each potential challenge is actually an opportunity. To test your strength. To learn a new skill. To embrace a new perspective.

With each new challenge I faced or new opportunity I was presented with, my dad would always remind me: "There is no such thing as failure as long as you are moving forward. As long as you're learning, in the end you're succeeding. True failure is not doing, not trying. So fail forward, and you'll always find yourself where you are supposed to be."

This forward momentum has always been my focus, from the very beginning. It has allowed me to take risks that others might have shied away

true failure is not doing, not trying.

from, with the knowledge that even if it didn't go according to plan, if I learned something from it I would come out ahead.

One of my most memorable early failures took place while I was still living in Texas—where local teens could come up with their own goods to sell at the local mall's Kids in Business Day. I was in junior high, and my sister, Kym, was in high school. Now she's a renowned photographer with a worldwide following across her social channels, and even at a young age, she was a talented creative whose artistry and craftsmanship inspired me. So we came up with an idea for a business selling bookmarks and greeting cards; my sister would design them, and we would sell them for twenty-five cents each. We spent weeks preparing for the event, crafting thoughtful cards with beautiful illustrations, and spent hours on intricate designs for each bookmark. We set up our table and displayed our creations with love.

Unfortunately, one by one, people bypassed our table to reach the one next to us. That table was filled with baked goods: brownies, cookies, and chocolate cake. They had a higher price ($1 per baked good) and much higher demand. The girls running the baked goods business eventually sold out, while we still had a table full of bookmarks and greeting cards that we had to pack up and take home with us at the end of the day.

Despite my initial surprise that

our business had "failed," the more I thought about it, the more it made sense, and the more I began to think about the other girls' "business plan." The girls had indicated, as they celebrated their victorious day, that they had just gone to the supermarket and picked up a few boxes of Duncan Hines brownie mix. So I went to the store to determine how much they had spent on their "product." Sure enough, when I found the baking aisle, I saw that each box cost $1–$2 and produced roughly twenty baked goods. Since they charged $1 per item, that meant they had made $20 from what had cost them just $1–$2 to buy. That was roughly $18 of profit per box.

My investigation continued. If they had sold two hundred baked goods that day, they had brought in $200 and spent only $10–$20 on the boxes of mix; in total, they had made $180–$200 in profit. Plus, they hadn't spent weeks like Kym and I had preparing for that day, instead investing only a few hours in the kitchen.

Now, I'm not saying that you shouldn't invest in the creation of a good product. But it got me thinking of how to create a business that could generate profit, so that I could later use those profits to further grow the business. While our greeting cards and bookmarks were beautiful, they clearly weren't in demand.

That failure taught me that you can have a great product and still fail. It doesn't mean your product is worthless, but you maybe need to refine your approach. And you should always do your market research and the math before you plan any business endeavor.

It was my first lesson in profit margins and marketability, even though I didn't know those business terms at the time, and I was determined not make the same mistakes next time. For the next few months, whenever our family would go to the grocery store, I would stroll along the baked goods section, studying those Duncan Hines boxes. I couldn't wait to show myself and the world what I had learned and how I had improved.

Unfortunately, we moved away from that local mall before I had a chance to redeem myself! But I'll never forget the lessons that failure taught me. I've applied the willingness to fail and the excitement to learn and improve to every business endeavor since then.

If I had been successful my first time around, I'm not sure that I would have learned any lessons. I would have

you have to be willing to fail, or you'll never try anything new.

IT'S NOT PERSONAL

We all fail. Every single one of us. The question is, How do you recover from your failures? Do you let it define you, and fear going big next time around? Or do you take stock of what went wrong and move forward, after learning some important lessons?

There is nothing wrong with you. Failure isn't even always about you. So long as you worked hard and tried your best, it can be due to the situation, the people you were competing with, or something that happened that knocked you off course. Don't let the failure determine how you feel about yourself. You'll have another chance.

thought I was just naturally good at business. Failure stings in the moment, but it serves you in the end and makes you that much better.

Anytime you try something new, there is always a chance you will fail. If you aren't willing to fail, you will never take a risk. And risk-taking is required if you are going to aim for great things.

Sometimes it helps to be willing to fail at small things first. My junior year of high school, I decided I wanted to learn the piano. Now, I had been studying violin for years and was first chair in the orchestra. But there was something about the piano that really attracted me. Jazz singer Norah Jones's "Don't Know Why" was especially popular at this time, and I desperately wanted to learn how to play that song and more.

Most people start an instrument when they are much younger than fifteen. And I had to start at the beginning, with simple songs like "Row, Row, Row

Your Boat." I was playing Mozart on the violin, but the equivalent of elementary school music on the piano. But no matter how good you are at one thing, you will often be a novice at something else. I knew that since I had learned violin, if I dedicated myself to the piano I could be excellent at it as well.

By the end of my first year of study, I entered the Dallas annual piano competition. Each musician was to prepare the same piece by Claude Debussy: "Doctor Gradus ad Parnassum." You would then come in and play for the judges, and they would rank and honor the top four pianists in Dallas, among the hundreds of competitors.

I hadn't performed in front of anyone before, and I knew that I was *way* less experienced than all the other musicians. I had started just a year before, after all! But I knew I could continue to practice harder than anyone. I got a recording of the piece of music and listened to it over and over. I practiced for hundreds of hours.

The day of the competition, I walked into the audition, sat down at the piano, and began to play.

A few measures in, I stopped. I couldn't remember the rest.

I clenched my fists, and my heart started to race. *What was I thinking, that I could pretend to be as skilled as all these other musicians?*

But I took a deep breath. I visualized my parents, and their courage and composure. And I started again.

This time, I played it the best that I ever had, better than in any of my practice sessions.

As the honors were announced, I was declared the fourth-place award winner. My near-perfect score when I played the piece the second time around helped me to clinch a top spot.

So the next time someone comes up to you with an offer to try something new, take it from me and say yes! Run for student government, or try out for debate, or run your church's food drive, or lead the mission trip. It's those things that scare us that help us grow the most. Failure is always a possibility. But you have to be willing to fail; otherwise you will never try anything new. And if you never try anything new, you'll never know how capable you are. You limit your growth and your potential when you think you have to know everything before taking on a new role or trying to develop a new skill.

RESISTING THE PURSUIT OF PERFECTION

Unfortunately, outside Silicon Valley, we don't often receive the message that failure is okay and, in fact, expected. Instead, we pursue perfection. We don't take a risk, because we are afraid of failing. We delay sharing something, because we think it isn't ready. We don't realize that sometimes we need to put our ideas out there, in their imperfect state, and that they will be perfected over time.

When I first launched Mogul, I knew that it was imperfect. I was not a graphic designer. And while I, luckily, had an older sister who was a photographer and who allowed me to use her images on the site, Mogul had a very rudimentary design when I first sent

RISK-TAKING 101

Weigh the opportunity.

What is the worst that can happen? Would you be okay if that actually came to pass? If the answer is yes, it is worth the risk.

Be prepared to work hard.

Every time you take a risk, you want to go into it hoping for success. You know that failure is an option, but don't plan on it. You work your tail off, so that even if you fail, you've given it everything you had.

Don't live with regret.

Step up to the moment. Speak up and volunteer for the opportunity or raise your hand for that job. You don't want to ever look back and wonder: *What if?*

it out. In fact, I sometimes laugh about how simple and "ugly" Mogul once was—but I was, and still am, so proud of that first design; after all, I created it with my own two hands. It is also a testament to how far we have come. You can waste precious time pursuing perfection. If I had waited until Mogul was perfect, I may never have taken that leap and sent it out into the world! Perfection is an illusion anyway—nothing is ever truly perfect. Everything can be improved upon. In fact, I was recently honored to have Melinda Gates say: "Take it from Mogul founder Tiffany Pham. If you want to build the perfect business, start with an imperfect idea."

What are you holding back on in hopes that you'll achieve perfection first? Do you refuse to perform an instrument in public, afraid that you'll make a mistake? Do you keep your writing to yourself? Do you fail to raise your hand and offer your solutions because you're afraid of ridicule, or scared that your idea will be rejected?

We have to take risks if we want to get what we want. And, yes, sometimes

you will fail, sometimes spectacularly! But you know what? You can always get back up again. You can let that fall define your future—or you can laugh it off, see what you learned from it, and try again.

LEARNING TO PIVOT THROUGH REJECTION

In 2017, I was invited to appear on the TLC reality show *Girl Starter*. Produced by Al Roker, it was a *Project Runway*–type show focused on female entrepreneurs. They wanted me to come on board as a mentor and judge.

I had worked on films before, but

I NEVER THOUGHT I'D BE ON REALITY TV.

always behind the scenes. I had never been "the talent," and the thought made me nervous. I knew that there would be no script. Even though they assured me that the scenes were set and that they would give me some guidelines on what to say, I knew that situations would arise in the moment and I would have to improvise.

But I loved the idea of being able to empower these women and also spread awareness of what Mogul was doing.

So despite my potential nerves, I said yes.

I remember how I had to consciously keep myself calm on that first day of filming. But I knew that I could do it, that with practice I would get better, even if that first day was a verified disaster. I came ready to kill it in my favorite black dress and my signature red lips and black eyeliner. And I tried to stay focused: not on the cameras, but on the bold, brave young women in front of me. Women who had a dream, an idea, and wanted to share it with the world.

I tried my best, and luckily, the producers enjoyed what I had to say,

SEE THE "NO" AS A "NOT RIGHT NOW"

The people who can keep going despite rejection understand something essential: There is no such thing as a "no," just a "not right now." Don't let "no" be the final answer. Try again in a few months, and you may get a different answer. Or start pursuing something else, and you may see the opportunity you were hoping for approach *you* this time around.

In fact, I don't even remember the nos I received, because I always focus on the yeses. When you get a no, try to see why that door may have closed. There might be a much more obvious opportunity right around the corner. And if you pursue that opportunity and get a yes, then you'll forget all about the no. Believe me.

OVERCOMING
FEAR

I get it—it is hard to feel fearful and move forward anyway. But I really believe in not having regrets. When you allow fear to hold you back, you have episodes in your life that you look back on and wonder: *What would have happened if I had possessed the courage to accept that challenge?* So here are a few concrete tips for overcoming fear.

Ask yourself: *How might I regret letting fear win, down the road?* Usually, just thinking about that gives me the boost to raise my hand, walk in the door, or force the words out of my throat. I just don't want to be someone who regrets things.

Think of someone who inspires you. It could be your parents (that's who I thought of during that piano competition), or it could be an icon like Audrey Hepburn or Eleanor Roosevelt, or it could be a modern-day leader like Sheryl Sandberg. Think of their grace, their courage, or their willingness to do unconventional things. For me, when I first saw Sheryl Sandberg speak, she was so warm, kind, and openhearted that I still think of her when I need to be inspired to be true to myself even when I'm feeling pressured to conform to someone else's expectations. When I'm speaking in public and I feel a case of nerves swoop over me, I think of my dad, who is a powerful orator, and try and channel a bit of his confidence. Having these touchstones in times of trial can help you keep going and push past the fear.

Develop a mantra that you say when fear arises. It could be something as simple as: "I can do this!" Or a quote from a writer that you love, like this one from Dale Carnegie: "Fear doesn't exist anywhere except in the mind." I truly believe in the power of positive thinking. Having a phrase that you return to, that you believe deep in your bones, that you say either in your head or out loud when you are feeling fearful, can help you move forward in a powerful way.

DRAWING INSPIRATION FROM SHERYL SANDBERG, A SUPPORTER OF MOGUL.

because they invited me to return for a second season!

I ended up loving the experience with the contestants on the show. I not only continue to mentor the winners as they build their company together but I've stayed in touch with the runners-up. One runner-up, in particular, was so talented, yet she struggled throughout the competition with communicating her ideas. An engineer, she is a very technical person, and would focus on those aspects of her idea when pitching. But connecting with the person you are pitching to and telling a story about your company is as important as how your product actually works. Throughout the season, I had been mentoring her: *You need to practice your storytelling. Think about the person you are talking to. What are they going to get out of this? Emotionally connect with them. Tell them the big picture of why you are doing this.*

And while she greatly improved over the course of the show, she did not go on to win *Girl Starter.*

A few months after the finale, she reached out to me. She'd been inspired by my path and was now applying to graduate school. She asked if I would be willing to look over her essays.

Of course I said yes. And once I started reviewing, I saw a similar problem: a focus on the minute details and a lack of big-picture storytelling. I helped guide her essays in the right direction, and when she got an interview, I guided her through that process as well,

ASK FOR FEEDBACK

Don't be afraid to get feedback, whether positive or negative. Feedback on your essay, your idea, your performance, leads you to address weaknesses you didn't know were there and get even better. There is no such thing as perfect. Everything can improve. Ask for feedback everywhere and anywhere you can!

A few questions to ask:

How could I connect with you better?

Is there anything you would change about what I just shared?

Do you have any tips on how I might present even better the next time?

coaching her and helping her improve how she was communicating her story, her "why."

To my great excitement, she ended up getting into Harvard Business School and happily accepted.

I was so proud. I was glad that she didn't let not winning *Girl Starter* derail her dreams. She knew how to pivot, to take stock of the moment and see what other opportunities might arise.

This is the art of failing forward: taking any setback you might have and figuring out a way to spin it into gold. Can you, like the entrepreneurs of Silicon Valley, tell a story where this failure was just one more step to success?

Create a story line about the event, the "failure," that explains the mistake or highlights the lesson you learned through it. That puts a positive spin on it. I love to create story lines about everything—my business, my career, even my relationship history. Creating a narrative that makes sense to you, and allows you to feel empowered, lets you be the author of your own story. This is a great skill to have when applying to college, internships, or jobs. You highlight the journey that you know you are

on, and you invite that organization to be a part of your story.

When you know how to fail forward, you have the confidence to acknowledge the truth while simultaneously using that situation to learn a lesson, pivot into something else, and continue pursuing your Girl Mogul dreams.

THE FAILURE FLIP

You failed at something. There's nothing you can do to change the past, but you can change the future by asking yourself these questions:

What did you learn from the experience?

What would you do differently next time?

What will you think about this experience in five years?

mogul mentor
NASTIA LIUKIN
OLYMPIC GOLD MEDALIST AND ENTREPRENEUR

When I was just eighteen years old, I achieved my lifelong dream: Olympic gold (in the women's gymnastics individual all-around)! And I thought that would be the pinnacle of my life and career. It really doesn't get any better than working for something your entire life and then actually achieving it.

But I was wrong. Because it was actually in the midst of my most public failure that I felt the most love, support, and joy that I've ever experienced.

It was four years later, and I was trying to make the Olympic team for the second time.

I mounted the bar for my routine, and then twenty seconds in I found myself lying face-flat on the mat. Needless to say, my Olympic dreams were over. Within just twenty seconds, my life had changed. It was time to move on. But

NASTIA LIUKIN

©Nastia Liukin

first, I needed to finish my bar routine. As I got up, finished the routine, and landed my dismount, twenty thousand people rose to their feet. I looked around in disbelief. The first standing ovation of my entire career. But why? Why were they on their feet for the worst routine of my life? That's when it hit me . . .

For so many years I had a fear of not being loved or supported if I didn't win the gold medal or succeed. In that moment, everything changed. When I looked around and saw twenty thousand people loving and supporting me in what I thought was the worst moment of my life, my eyes filled with tears. Emotions overtook my entire body.

And this is what became the defining moment of my entire career. Five Olympic medals, nine world championship medals, and an ESPY Award didn't give me the feeling I had in San Jose that summer.

Don't get me wrong; when I won the gold medal four years prior it was an amazing moment. It taught me that hard work pays off. If you set a goal or dream and work hard every single day, anything is possible. But the moment I had four years *later*, made me realize so much more about life. That through the ups and downs, successes and failures, people would still love and support me no matter what color medal I received (or didn't receive).

And when I got up on the beam just a few minutes later, I knew it was the last time I would be performing on the world stage in that way. And I performed my routine as I never had before, fully soaking up every single moment of it.

It was like I could say goodbye because I knew it was over.

If I hadn't made such a huge mistake on the bars, I might have missed that moment. And it was a beautiful moment.

So failure can be the greatest gift. It really can. As long as you can go someplace positive afterward, it's not really failure. It's just one door closing as another one opens. ⌣

PART TWO

Choose your team.

CHAPTER FIVE
FINDING YOUR PEOPLE

No matter how smart you are, how confident you feel, and how dedicated you are to your goal, you'll never get where you want to go on your own.

Think about what Mogul is at its heart. It is a community. It is a huge group of women coming together to support and mentor one another. I truly believe that when you find your people—the ones who encourage you to be the best version of yourself, the ones who encourage you to go after your dreams, the ones who are willing to drop everything and support you when you need it—that is when you will start living your Girl Mogul life.

And why would you want to do it on your own? It is so much sweeter when you achieve success with friends, family, and collaborators by your side.

It's not always easy to find your people. I began to make the kinds of friends who would push me forward instead of drag me down only when I got to high school. Before that, I'd made

friends out of necessity. I wanted people to sit with at lunch and hang out with after school. I was never alone, but that didn't mean I wasn't lonely. The queen bee of the popular group I joined in middle school was a bully. After being subjected to her ridicule a few times, I realized I'd much rather sit alone.

BEFRIEND PEOPLE YOU WANT TO BE

I've learned throughout the years that the best way to make friends is out of admiration, not desperation. Having no friends is better than bad friends. Who you surround yourself with impacts your mood, self-esteem, and what you believe is possible in the world.

When I met Diane in high school and witnessed her excelling in math (and just about everything else, honestly), I admired her, followed her example, and, in the process, we became friends. Knowing her led me to become a better version of myself, because I saw someone who was smart, working hard, and committed to doing her best. It was contagious.

When I got to college, I met Susannah. She was well-liked on campus, and well-regarded for her creative endeavors. Susannah was constantly creating, coming up with new projects, and introducing new ideas to students. Plus, I loved the way she carried herself. She was always kind and generous. No matter who you were, she had a kind word to share with you. No matter how busy she was, she would take the time to check in.

Susannah opened up a whole new world of friends for me. Though I was actively trying to push myself out of my shyness at the beginning of my college years, I know that I would have continued to struggle if I hadn't met Susannah. She introduced me to new friends and opportunities, always thinking so highly of me when I wasn't always thinking highly of myself. In fact, because of the friends I met through Susannah, I was tapped to join

one of Yale's secret societies.

But it was her friendship that I cared about most. We were both interested in working in media and entertainment. She wanted to hear about what it was like to work on the *Herald*. I loved hearing her talk about her plan to go to film school one day and the possibility of the two of us doing something together in that industry.

Susannah and I were always so happy for each other and supportive of anything the other did. I truly felt like I had a friend who was there for me no matter what, no questions asked. And our close friendship has continued in this way, long past college.

Susannah was one of the first people who taught me how powerful it can be to collaborate on projects with your friends. We collaborated on the *Misfit*, the literary magazine that she founded and that I went on to become publisher of after my time at the *Herald*. After graduation, she went to film school, where she thrived, but she was struggling to find financing for one particular film called *Hermit*. I was at

CBS at the time, but I stepped in, in the evenings after my full-time job, to help her find financing and distribution, and we successfully raised the remaining amount of the budget needed. The film was eventually nominated for an HBO Audience Award, and Susannah named me as a producer alongside her, as thanks for going above and beyond.

But I was thankful to her. This was yet another time I'd experienced how powerful it could be to do important work with someone that you cherish. Our friendship and subsequent collaboration became the model for how I would partner with people going forward.

Friends can also be essential not just for opening doors to new opportunities but to help you stay true to yourself. When I enrolled in business school, I knew that finding a good friend would be essential to keeping my spirits up and my sense of humor intact as I entered classrooms and scenarios where I would be one of just a handful of women. Enter Stephanie. When our classmates asked who would be willing to help organize the food for our fall retreat up in the mountains of Vermont, we both raised our hands and, shortly after, found ourselves wandering the aisles of Costco together. Stephanie and I soon became valued sounding boards

STEPHANIE AND ME WITH OUR CLASSMATES AT HARVARD BUSINESS SCHOOL, ALREADY THE BEST OF FRIENDS.

and confidants for each other during the two years we were at HBS.

Stephanie had been an engineering major at Purdue, so she was already very familiar with being one of the only women in a field dominated by men. She showed me that you don't have to change who you are to fit in. We both ended up being known as the "nice girls" in our class. In business, sometimes, as a woman you are encouraged to *not* be nice. You are pressured into thinking that you need to adopt more "masculine" airs as a way of proving that you belong there. And men, quite frankly, aren't taught that they need to be nice. Therefore, the stereotype of a female HBS graduate was brash, unemotional, and unwavering.

But Stephanie reminded me that I could stay true to who I was. I had an example in front of me of a woman forging her own path to success and staying strong in her conviction that she didn't need to change to be accepted. Having Stephanie by my side allowed me to stick to being authentically kind, warm, and empathetic at all times.

Friends shouldn't just be people that you socialize with but people who help shape who you are and who you're becoming. When you surround yourself with people who you think you can learn from, who will encourage the best out of you, who allow you to be yourself, you feel empowered. When you're surrounded by people who drag you down, you fight twice as hard to get to where you want.

FIND A TRUE SUPPORTER

Who you choose to have by your side as a romantic partner is just as essential to your success as having supportive girlfriends. I've had a number of relationships, and each one taught me a valuable lesson, one that was totally necessary even if it was painful at the time. I've learned that no one should be forced to choose between a romantic relationship and pursuing their dreams. Lady Gaga famously said: "Some women choose to follow men, and some women choose to follow their dreams. If you're wondering which way to go, remember that your career will never wake up and tell you that it doesn't love you anymore."

I didn't really date until college. I was way too shy in junior high to even hold a guy's hand (sorry, J), and even in high school, I was so focused on school, activities, and friends that I didn't feel like anything was missing. I know some people have plenty of relationships in their high school years. And that's great! As long as who you date meets the same standards we set for your friends. Are they encouraging you to be the best version of yourself? Are they someone you want to be like? Do they make you dream bigger and believe in yourself more?

If the answer is no, then think about whether they are really worth your time.

I met my first boyfriend, W, after I graduated from Yale and he graduated from Princeton. He was so handsome, popular, and athletic that I struggled to believe that he even liked me. I thought: *There must be some mistake. He can't really like me, can he?* Due to that insecurity, I focused on being the perfect girlfriend. In fact, I was so focused on being the perfect girlfriend that I forgot to be myself.

It's not like I was putting on an act, but I didn't ever tell him how I was really feeling deep inside. One of the things we were both proud of at the time is that we never fought during our two-year relationship. Now I know why that was! We never fought because I never shared how I truly felt, just to avoid any conflict. A perfect girlfriend would agree with everything he said and never feel disappointed, right? I know now that conflict is a necessary part of any relationship, because if you aren't experiencing any conflict, you probably aren't truly communicating. And if you aren't truly communicating, why are you even in a relationship?

You have to be able to be yourself. Hold out for someone who is ready and willing to embrace your real, flawed self.

My second relationship, with S, taught me how important it is to have someone who supports your ambitions

GIRL SQUAD
CHECK-IN

Who are some of your closest friends? What are a few attributes that you admire most about them? If you can't think of anything you admire about them, take a moment to think about how they encourage you or bring out the best in you. And if there's still nothing positive coming to mind, ask yourself if they are truly the kind of support system you need in your life.

If you find yourself in need of some new additions to your girl squad, here are some tips for making new friends:

Look for people who possess the qualities you desire to develop in yourself. Then take note of the activities these girls are involved in. Try to join something they are a part of so that you can get to know them in a natural setting, whether it is decorating the float for the homecoming parade, volunteering for a fundraiser, or helping out with teacher appreciation week.

Use social media to your advantage. If you see a post from a friend of a friend on social media that speaks to you, comment on it! Support their endeavors and start a friendship online. That can then extend into real life once you've already had some exchanges in the virtual world.

> **Join a team.** Some of the best friendships can be cultivated when you are working together toward a common goal. So think about joining a sports team, a choir, trying out for the play, or joining the debate team. These activities will not only expose you to new people but will also give you the chance to develop new skills. A win-win for everyone!

and isn't threatened by your success. We began dating a few years after college graduation, while I was in business school. And we were great together for a while. I then started working at CBS, while he pursued a career in finance.

But finance wasn't what S really wanted to be doing. It was something he thought he should pursue because it was a lucrative field. His passions, though, were in writing and teaching.

I tried to encourage him to find a way back to what he truly loved. But S didn't listen. And as I began to pursue my dream of building my own company, he started to get resentful. When he learned I was teaching myself to code, he would make fun of me, mimicking

the way I typed, hunched over a keyboard. He thought my dreams were impractical, unreachable—that all my hard work would be a waste.

But I knew Mogul was what I wanted to commit my life to.

We broke up the night I launched the company. S told me I had to choose between Mogul and our relationship. I think he saw how much of myself I was going to be giving to my new company, and he didn't want to have to compete for my time.

Crushed, I chose Mogul.

So in those months when I was launching the company, I was also nursing a broken heart. And that wasn't easy. It was lonely and sad but also incredibly

WATCH OUT FOR THESE PHRASES!

The following are code words for *Your ideas are silly*:

• Stop thinking you're so important.

• Focus on me.

• Stop going after your dreams.

But when you start to hear the following from someone who claims to really like you, whether as a love interest or as a friend, it is time to bail:

• Why do you need to have that hobby? Just spend time with me.

• Ditch your friends. They aren't that cool anyway.

• Blow it off! You don't need to study for that test.

• Who cares? It isn't that important.

• Who do you think you are? You're young. Just have fun! You can work hard later.

you have to be able to be yourself.

should ever ask you to give up on your dreams.

Some people aren't going to love how ambitious you are. But if they are threatened by your dreams or what you hope to accomplish someday, they aren't the person for you. There are plenty of people out there who do love ambitious women. Find one of them. Find a true supporter and sounding board, someone who has dreams of their own and isn't intimidated by what you have to offer the world—just as I've found in my incredible partner now, named C.

DON'T BE AFRAID TO DEPEND ON YOUR FAMILY

I've always known I have a soft place to land no matter what I have been going through, thanks to my family. They are my rock, my starting point, and the place I'm always going to come back to. During the first few months of Mogul's existence, my parents flew to New York and stayed with me. They were always in the kitchen, making me comforting

exciting. I knew that Mogul would be with me for a lifetime. S would one day become a distant memory—at least that's what I told my heart. Eventually, I could see that he taught me a valuable lesson about relationships: No one bowls of phở, or sitting at the dining room table, testing out the next iteration of Mogul. They were Mogul's first users but most important to me, my true supporters.

If you have a reliable and helpful family, don't be afraid to lean on them. Go to your parents with your goals and talk to them about different opportunities that might allow you to reach them faster. Bring them on as partners and strategize together on how you might go after what you want. While you are still living in their household, things will go much smoother if you have their support and cooperation. And here's a hint: Most parents love to encourage their child's dreams and will even sacrifice some of their own happiness to help achieve them!

If you aren't fortunate enough to have immediate family members who will join you in your endeavors, think about people you have in your life who could fill this role. Maybe it is someone from your extended family, or a neighbor, a teacher, or a guidance counselor. Find people you look up to who can help

you with applications or interviews, and to just be someone to listen when you discuss future projects or ideas.

I've even formally welcomed my family onto Mogul's team. David, my brother, is our chief product officer and chief technology officer. He's a serial entrepreneur and highly sought-after technology leader in New York City, whose calm wisdom and philosophical manner is highly admired. While we didn't initially intend to work together, it was clear early on how much a part of the team he was. In those early days of Mogul's explosive growth, he would swoop in and save the day anytime the site crashed. He is brilliant, and at the time, he was

WITH MY BROTHER DAVID, LEADING THE EARLY TEAM AT MOGUL.

Audrey Froggatt

considering launching his own startup while simultaneously consulting for a number of companies. But as he watched Mogul's growth, he kept stepping in and getting involved. By the time we had offices at The Yard, he was coming in three to four times a week. Ultimately, he and I both knew that as one of the company's founders, he should join Mogul full-time.

I can't tell you how amazing it is to go to work each day with my brother. We've always gotten along; I respect him greatly. But what I love most about having him on my team is how much I trust him. He always has my, and the company's, best interests at heart. Leading the development of our mobile app, web, and mobile web platforms, as well as new products and innovations, he guides the team at Mogul as much as I do. He is one of our most beloved team members due to his kindness and warmth, and everyone knows they can depend on him for emotional support and intellectual collaboration.

Obviously, your family is important when you are growing up, but I'm not afraid to lean on my family even now. They are the backbone of who I am, and checking back in with them, staying connected with them, allows me to feel the most connected with myself. Leaning on family allows you to know when you need help, who you can turn to when you need it, and to recognize that sometimes we all just need a little love that only our friends and family can provide.

CREATE YOUR OWN TEAM

My success has come not just from good friends who set forth a positive example, who encouraged me to be myself, and from family who always cheered me on. It has also come from a pattern of identifying the people whom I knew I could count on, and who, when we joined together, allowed me to accomplish more than I could on my own.

From the start, I knew that Mogul was bigger than me and that I needed to have the right people around to help it grow into its potential. My Mogul family was created with my very first hires.

In addition to my brother, I hired an NYU marketing graduate intern named Namisha, who stepped in when it was just me, in my sweatpants. I would meet her at Argo Tea in Columbus Circle, in hopes that she wouldn't realize I was still working from my bedroom. Even though she was technically just an intern, Namisha brilliantly grabbed hold of every single social media channel, our emails, and our other forms of communication with the outside world, and helped shape Mogul into the worldwide marketing powerhouse that it is today. She is now SVP of global marketing and spearheads Mogul Redefined, our consumer products division, which develops innovative, cutting-edge educational products for our users. Namisha is proof that you should never let your age or your title prevent you from taking something on and absolutely showing your value.

Bethany was someone I met while I was at business school and she was at Juilliard. We were connected through a mutual mentor named Rob, who had a prophecy that we would be great collaborators. As soon as we met, we began to pull each other into different initiatives we were working on, producing synergies for both. Mogul was my biggest initiative to date, so Bethany was next to come on board. Today, she is VP of global content.

Juli, whom I met through my ex-boyfriend S (we joke that she was the best thing I got out of that relationship!), became a super-user of Mogul and reached out in hopes that she could step in and help with anything we needed. She did that and more. She rolled up her sleeves and built our entire infrastructure internally (from legal and accounting to culture and talent) so that we could grow externally. She is now SVP of global people operations.

Natasha was someone I met through her older brother, who I'd worked with, and she and I had been meeting together for years. When she reached out to see how she could support Mogul, I realized that there was an avenue for growth that would be

SHARING THE STORY OF MOGUL DURING THE OPENING KEYNOTE IN AUSTRIA.

perfectly tailored to Natasha's skill sets and background. She led the development of our Mogul Learning courses, and today is VP of global sales and partner success.

These were the people I depended on in those early days, when Mogul was growing so quickly, and we were shaping where it would head. Mogul would not be where it is today without them. No matter what stage of life you're in, when you surround yourself with people that you trust and that you value having by your side, you escalate your growth and your enjoyment along the way. I've definitely met people who struggled with trusting others with their ideas. They don't want to let go of control, and thus they miss out on the opportunity to collaborate with others. I have actually loved the act of letting go of certain aspects of running Mogul, of determining the people I trust inherently and watching them excel beyond what I could have done on my own.

When you are finding your people, it is also an acknowledgment that you can't know and do everything yourself. When I launched Mogul, I reached out to advisors like Cathie Black, former chairman and president of Hearst Magazines; Ann Sarnoff, president of BBC Studios Americas; and Jarrod Dicker, former head of product, strategy, and technology at the *Washington Post*. These were trusted mentors who I knew had strategic insights from decades of experience that I did not have, people who could not only help guide me during important decision-making but also could bring even more validity to Mogul when we sought investors. We all have certain skill sets, and you cannot be perfect at everything right away. Finding your people means recognizing your weaknesses and thinking about who you could meet with to help you gain knowledge, experience, and expertise in those areas.

I created Mogul so that women everywhere can have access to this kind of support. So they can reach out to one another for advice and ideas. So that they can ask whatever they want of a luminary. So they can be further mentored when they sign up for our Mogul Learning courses. So they can realize that when we come together, we are stronger than when we stand alone.

When you find your people, you feel fully supported and ready to take risks and go after what you want. Don't feel like you need to act alone. Build a team of people that can help you do everything you want and more.

CREATE A BOARD OF ADVISORS FOR YOUR LIFE

There is no reason that a board of advisors should exist only for nonprofits and businesses. You can create your own team of advisors, people you turn to for advice in certain areas of your life. Who will be your go-to people when you find yourself getting into unhealthy habits? Who can you turn to when you need to discuss relationship woes? Who will be your sounding board for what kind of activities to pursue or lessons to take?

Think of those you look up to who would potentially be available and dependable with their advice. The people on this list can be adults or they can be peers whom you respect. Think of teachers, coaches, former babysitters, and camp counselors. Let them know you value their influence on your life and that you'd like to be able to come to them from time to time—and that you would love to support and give back to them, too.

It can be a bit intimidating to make that first move of approaching someone to be a mentor or advisor. But just go for it, because I promise you that most people will be greatly honored and more than happy to step in and become an advisor for your life.

Write down at least one person you would like to reach out to for the following areas of your life:

- **Health**
- **Relationships**
- **High school**
- **College**
- **Career**
- **Extracurricular activities**
- **Volunteering and philanthropy**
- **Saving and managing money**

Here is a simple template for reaching out:

Dear X,

I hope you are well. I'm currently trying to set my sights higher when it comes to what I can achieve, and I am creating a kind of board of advisors for my life, so that when I face a decision or need some advice, I know exactly who I can turn to. I would love for you to join my team. I have watched how skillfully you manage your X, and thus was wondering if you would be willing to be my go-to for all things X. I promise it won't be a huge tax on your time, and that I will contact you in advance to schedule dates that work best for you to either get together in person or communicate via phone.

Either way, thank you so much for being in my life.

Love,
Me

mogul mentor
PIERA GELARDI
COFOUNDER AND EXECUTIVE CREATIVE DIRECTOR OF REFINERY 29

I never knew exactly what my path in life would be, but I've always followed my intuition: to make one choice that felt right followed by another. The accumulation of those decisions, of trying things, responding, and recalibrating, has led me to where I am today.

PIERA GELARDI

Erin Yamagata

I think we spend so much time as girls and women being conditioned to worry about what other people think about us, but what matters most is what *you* think and what *you* want. Figuring out what you want takes time. I write in a journal every night, documenting the day, the highlights, lowlights, my triumphs, and things that could have gone better. Then a few times a month, I look through and notice the themes, take stock, and adjust. If nothing else, notice what lights you up.

Try to start the discipline now of regularly hitting the pause button, tuning into yourself, and exploring your motivations and desires. Some of those will stay constant throughout your life and some will change. Regular gut checks are critical!

As a girl growing up in Maine, I didn't see anyone that had the exact career for me. So I paid attention to what I did find compelling about the lives of the folks around me—my entrepreneur dad's curiosity and work ethic, my social worker mom's dedication to her community, the creative expression of the artists and makers my parents were friends with. I focused on the qualities I wanted to cultivate in myself and in my life.

I explored lots of different interests (even ones I knew wouldn't lead to a career), and that served me really well as an entrepreneur and creative (it's all in the mash-up). Playing sports taught me endurance and teamwork, doing theater built my confidence and ability to present ideas, and creative writing built my ability to tell stories. Pursuing your interests fuels any path you take.

When I was in high school, I did a summer program at the Rhode Island School of Design to pursue my passion for art, and it was there that I truly found *my people*. Folks that made me feel so seen, so inspired, so full of life. Surrounding yourself with supportive, inspiring people is critical for your development . . . You can build a chosen family in addition to the one you were born into.

When we were starting Refinery29, it was really grassroots, focused on independent designers and stores. Everyone said we wouldn't be successful because the stores and designers didn't have a lot of money. But that community supported us—our first ad was from an indie store in Brooklyn and our first investor was a designer with stores throughout the city. Building community is everything. When I think about some of the most game-changing artists, many of them were part of a community that inspired each other and rose together as a movement.

My life now is a representation of the things I've sought out in the world—an eclectic mix of creative endeavors, thoughtful conversations, courageous decisions, and an extra dose of dancing—and while it seems aligned on the outside, it's taken a lot of self-discovery and trial and error to get here.

My mom once told me, "We're all works in progress. What matters most is putting in the work to progress." 👑

CHAPTER SIX
RISING ABOVE
(AKA LATER, HATERS)

It is thanks to bullies that Mogul exists. That's right. The seeds of Mogul were first planted during the insecure years of junior high when I faced ridicule for being who I was.

While my goal of creating something like Mogul was established when my grandmother passed away, it was the feelings of self-doubt and unhappiness generated by girls focused on bringing people down that made me wonder why it was that girls were taught to compete with one another. It made me dream about a community that was supportive, encouraging, and loving.

Today, Mogul is the supportive network of friends that I wished I'd had growing up—but a million times bigger.

I'm not going to sugarcoat it: It can sometimes be difficult—really difficult—in middle school, high school, and even college to find a group of people who will accept you 100 percent for who you truly are. But what you *can* find are ways to funnel any negativity into

something positive. And if you can do this, the moment you hit rock bottom just might be the moment that makes your dreams take flight.

FEEL SECURE IN YOUR STRENGTHS (IT'S WHERE THEY'LL ATTACK FIRST)

No matter where you find yourself—about to face the harrowing halls of high school, or on the cusp of entering college—you are likely to encounter people who will want to exclude you, who seem to want to tear you down or spread rumors that have no shred of truth to them. But take it from me. You can use these attacks and funnel their negative energy into positive channels. Think about it: If you weren't awesome, they wouldn't be targeting you! So don't let negative attention destroy your self-esteem. Let it open your eyes to how relevant you are.

After several years of loneliness

when I first moved to Texas, I finally found a group of "friends" who seemed to welcome me into their ranks. I was thrilled to finally have someplace to sit in the cafeteria and was eager to join what I assumed would be an unconditionally supportive circle. Boy, was I in for a surprise! Three of them had created a book that they carried around school, in which they made fun of everyone in our class (yep, a real-life "burn book," straight out of *Mean Girls*).

They spent their days writing snarky comments in different-colored gel pens, gluing in unflattering photos, insulting people's looks, and spreading vicious rumors. At first, I brushed it off. But it turned out, the book had a page about me. The words mocked my jet-black hair, my friendliness, and my passion for school. I tried to pretend I hadn't seen anything. But I can't deny that deep inside I felt shame settling into the pit of my stomach. Not only were they writing mean comments about other people but they had taken things that I was proud of (I had always thought of my straight black hair as one of my best features) and tried to make me feel silly and stupid.

I soon stopped sitting with them at lunch and poured myself even more into school. At home, I tried to experience true friendship vicariously, through TV shows like *Friends* and *Gilmore Girls*, and movies like *Legally Blonde*. But that just made me feel more alone. The girls on the screen had friends to call on no matter what, friends who encouraged their ambitions and accepted them for who they were. Whereas outside of my family, I had no one.

When I graduated from middle school, I left my old "friends" behind without a second glance. I was fortunate to be able to do so because I lived in a neighborhood that was zoned to a different high school. I could finally escape those girls (who ever since I had decided not to be a part of their clique had found other ways to make me feel small, insignificant, and stupid). Socially, things started to turn around when I made friends with Diane, someone who was interested in the same things as I was, and wasn't afraid to be smart and work *each of us has something different to bring to the world.*

else, they make themselves feel more powerful. But that's not where power comes from.

I know I'm not the only one who faced a pack of mean girls growing up. By pushing one version of beauty and success, the media likes to pit girls against one another. But our value does not lie in how we look or who loves us. There is so much more to who we are than our outer shell, and each one of us brings something unique to the world. It can be hard to know that when you are young, but it becomes crystal clear as you get older. No two girls are exactly alike. Each of us has something different to bring to the world. So why would we ever try to compete with one another? Isn't it time we stop the competition and realize that when we stop tearing each other down, we can all rise up together?

If you are facing haters, know that you have a choice: You can let them win by allowing their words to make you question who you are. Or you can act like you are made of armor and let their words bounce right off. Easier said than

her hardest. That's when I finally realized what true friendship looks like.

Once I got to Yale, I realized that the qualities those girls had bullied me for, others viewed as strengths. I made friends who were engaged in their classes, passionate about world issues, and more concerned with books than looks. I began to realize that bullying, at its core, stems from insecurity. It stems from anxiety in the heart of the bully, and all too often the people being bullied are the ones the bullies most want to be like. By belittling someone done, I know. But every time you feel attacked, think about something that you know makes you stand out. Every time you feel belittled, think of something that makes you strong. Every time you feel mocked, check back in with who you truly are and who you know you are meant to be. They cannot demolish that person. If you don't let them in, you don't let them win.

Know that Mogul exists. If you need to find a place to vent, feel inspired, or find support, we are here for you. I created Mogul so that no girl will feel alone. So that every girl can find a community that gathers around her, encourages her, and lets her know that she can do more than anyone thought possible.

WHEN THE WHOLE WORLD SEEMS AGAINST YOU

While I'm so thankful that I've been able to create an online community like Mogul that can make you feel safe and supported, I also know that social media has created a world much more terrifying than any high school cafeteria. That for every way that social media allows people to feel more connected, it can also make them feel helplessly alone. Somehow people feel like they can behave online in ways they never would in public.

I know firsthand how even one small comment can make you feel like the whole world is against you.

During my senior year of college, I befriended a popular athlete who was also asked to join the Senior Class Council. He was friendly, handsome, and, of course, talented in his sport. And despite plenty of girls being interested, he had never really dated much. Many girls admitted they'd had crushes, and yet he kept to himself.

But around Thanksgiving of our senior year, he confided in some other players on his team: He liked me.

I had no idea that this at all mattered to anyone else until some strange messages appeared on my Facebook wall. It all started with a simple act of kindness. He had texted me that he was hungry and didn't know if he'd

HOW TO SHUT A BULLY DOWN
IN FIVE MINUTES OR LESS

Here's a trick I recently discovered that I wish I'd learned about years ago. It is a way to handle bullying or mean behavior that shifts the power dynamic immediately. It comes from Brooks Gibbs, an anti-bullying expert who travels to different high schools to speak with students about how to defuse bullying by refusing to engage in the fight. As I said, anyone who is bullying you or making fun of you is trying to knock you down a few pegs. Sociologists call it "dominance behavior." Your very existence challenges bullies in some way. Maybe they wish they could star in the play like you, or sing in the choir. Maybe they wish that guys befriended them the way they easily flock to you. So they are going to try to pass their insecurity on to you by saying something nasty.

But here's the trick. If you agree with whatever they say, they have nothing to push against. There is no way for them to "win" if you don't engage in the fight. Here's an example:

BULLY: You are so lame. Nice outfit!

YOU: Thanks!

BULLY: Um, okay. Well, I hope you have fun at your loser rehearsal tonight.

YOU: Oh man, yeah, it's a real time suck starring in the play. I wish I could just go home or hang out at the mall, too. You are so lucky!

Really, it works. Without the conflict, without fighting words back, there's no place for the bully to go—except away.

have time to get dinner before practice. And since I knew I'd be passing by Gourmet Heaven, I thought I'd pick something up for him. No big deal. I ordered "Sandwich #2" and left it at his door on my way out of town.

He was so appreciative, and we started texting every day. Of course, that's when it all came crashing down.

Upon returning to campus, I sat in my room reflecting on how this time period seemed to be one of those rare moments when everything was going well—from family to friends to academics. Then—I opened Facebook and saw one notification after another pop up. Strange. I checked my wall to see why everyone was talking to me.

This was before privacy settings on Facebook—when anyone could write on your wall. I saw a bunch of posts from people I didn't know well, making comments about whether I could get *them* a sandwich, that *they* were hungry, too—could they please get something delivered to *their* door?

My first reaction was confusion. How did they even know that I had

brought him a sandwich? And why would they care? Had he told them? Was he making fun of me, despite being so kind and considerate to my face?

While I didn't know what exactly had happened, I knew that I felt targeted and belittled. There were so many well-coordinated posts that it had clearly been thought through and carefully executed. It seemed calculated and designed to make me feel under attack. My hands shook as I hit DELETE on all these posts, only to see new ones spring up to take their place. I felt like I had a chorus of mean girls standing before me, taunting me. It took me straight back to junior high and those feelings of insecurity, and made me think that even though I strived to be nice to everyone, it didn't really matter.

I know now that it was just jealousy, and the girls were trying to get me to back off from the guy they were interested in. But in that moment, even though it was probably just one girl getting her friends to post, I was embarrassed and ashamed, even assuming that the athlete and his entire team, too, was involved. After that, I stopped talking to him and, in fact, hid from him for months, feeling like the butt of a cruel joke.

But the truth was: *He* hadn't been making fun of me at all. Some of his teammates had happened to tell the other girls about the sandwich in passing, by chance. Yet from the outside, things seemed so much worse than they actually were. That's often the case with bullying. You feel like the whole world is against you—when in fact, it's not. As it turned out, the athlete had come to my defense behind the scenes, and eventually those girls abandoned their interest in him. But the damage was done.

If I'd known back then what I know now, I wouldn't have let some silly comments on a website keep me so down that I could barely make it out of my room for months. It seems silly that I let people I didn't know dictate my behavior. But there is one thing I'm proud of. I never stooped to their level.

Even when I saw them on campus, months later, I always smiled, said hi, and didn't let them know that their actions got to me. In the end, it embarrassed them to know they'd hurt someone who was always nice to them.

Literally right before I stepped onstage to give the speech at graduation, the girls behind those Facebook posts stood before me and apologized, thanking me for the work I'd done for our college class.

Instead of letting the negativity spread, I'd stopped the cycle, moved on, and focused on how I could be kinder to those around me. I knew from that experience that I wanted to always be generous, and supportive of others, no matter what.

Facing that kind of negativity from my peers my final year in college also encouraged me to apply to business school. It made me realize that it was time to figure out how to build this company that had been brewing in my mind for years. It was time to funnel the pain to create a place where girls realized that there was a different way to go, where I could prevent this kind of thing from ever happening to others.

YOUR SOCIAL
MEDIA MANIFESTO

Listen, I get it—social media is a part of our lives. It can be an amazing force for good, but it can also be a pretty horrible place for your self-esteem. From dealing with FOMO when you watch people you thought were your friends have some amazing outing that they forgot to invite you to, to dealing with trolls who will hate on you for no reason except that you exist, here are some guidelines to keep you from getting sucked into the vortex of online harassment, image obsession, and bullying.

- Take a time-out. Give yourself one day a week when you don't even go on social media. Connect with people in person, go outside, and remember how sweet it is to be with people IRL!

- When someone bullies you online, use the same tactic mentioned earlier: agree with them, in a lighthearted way. You know what they're saying isn't true. Really, they know it isn't true. Don't fight them or get sucked into an online battle. Or just ignore it. They are often looking for a fight, and after a lack of engagement they often just move on.

- Understand your intention in sharing on social media. Are you trying to connect with friends and/or family? Show a window into your life for those who aren't with you? Be mindful of how your post could be perceived. If you are with some good friends but you know that one of your other buddies might have wished to be included, do you need to post? Finally, always be aware of how a post might be perceived by a potential employer. This is getting to be more and more important, so be thoughtful about how you present yourself in all public profiles.

- Maintain your own sense of self. I know it's hard, but don't compare yourself with others. Each person is completely unique, with different passions, callings, and backgrounds. There is only one you. Think about who you are and what makes you special, and then refine and reflect that in your postings. Are you someone who likes to post thoughtful musings that make people stop and think? Do you like to spread positivity? Are you impassioned about causes and eager to tell people about them? Do you love fashion and style, and like sharing how you refine your personal appearance day by day?

So in some ways, I have to thank those girls for their Facebook posts. It's thanks to experiences like these that I found the courage to step out and do something scary. I had to. For the next generation to come. Because I knew there was a better way.

KNOW WHEN TO LISTEN AND WHEN TO LET IT GO

Though there will be a time when you finally graduate out of the kinds of social situations that breed bullies, it's impossible to keep all negativity from arising in your life—especially if you are trying to do something out of the box, something that challenges people's perceptions of who you should be or what you should be doing. This is particularly true if you are trying to build a business. People like the status quo, so when you come to them with a different way of approaching a problem or a unique way of structuring your company, you might receive some pushback. Thankfully, when we first approached investors for Mogul, we encountered a ton of support from people willing to take a chance on our vision and mission. But there were many others who wanted to steer us in a different direction.

Early on in Mogul's growth, when I was still calling potential investors from my bedroom, I talked to a woman who initially, when she had reviewed the numbers, sounded incredibly excited and like it was a done deal. But the more I talked about what I envisioned Mogul becoming, a place where women across the world could share insights and ideas from the ground up, and would therefore be in control of what was on our platform in real time, she began to voice reservations.

"Well, I'm more interested in traditional media," she said, "where Mogul is a publishing company, in control of the content, and has a certain voice and viewpoint. This way, there is more creative control."

As I continued to advocate for our mission and vision, explaining that this would be a community for women worldwide, I realized that there was a clear misalignment. She didn't truly partake in our passion and idea.

So I politely thanked her for her time and hung up the phone. Sure, I was disappointed to lose this investor. But I could not alter our team's entire vision for our company just because one person disagreed. I wasn't going to abandon our fundamental reason for creating this platform. I wanted women to learn from one another, lnot from me!

I'm not saying that you shouldn't listen to feedback. But if someone's feedback challenges the very reason for what you arc doing, it is always better to stay true to yourself and move forward with your passion intact. For us, going with that one investor's fccdback would have completely changed the direction of the company.

If you are still in the nascent stages of envisioning what you aim to create or put forth into the world, or what you want to pursue, negative feedback can be helpful. It could guide you in the right direction. But check in with your gut. If someone is telling you something that doesn't feel right to you, let it go. If they are pushing you toward a summer job that doesn't inspire you or a class they think is absolutely vital to your future, but *you* can't stand the idea, you are allowed to let it go. You are the only expert on you, and you are the only one who knows what it is that you truly desire to create in the world.

Trust yourself, first and foremost.

STAYING STRONG

Facing haters is never the most enjoyable part of life, but it can serve you well by strengthening your self-esteem, fortifying your resolve, and renewing your commitment to be a force of support and kindness in the world.

Shortly after Mogul's meteoric rise, I received a message from one of my middle school bullies via Facebook.

The message read:

Hi Tiffany!

I've been randomly thinking of you lately with all the anti-bullying campaigns, and I just really wanted to apologize for my actions and contributions to making Plano such a crappy place to be. It's been on my mind for years now to be honest, and I never had the guts to tell you that I've been ashamed of my actions. So please know that I am not the same person, and it is a huge regret of mine.

On a brighter note, I am about to finish up a degree in May, but besides that, nothing huge has been going on in my life unlike you! I am so proud that I know someone as ambitious as you, and I am so happy to see that you are living life to the fullest. If you are ever in Dallas, please do let me know.

Wishing you ALL the best.

I stared at the screen in dismay, but also with gratitude. Even after all she had done, I had forgiven and forgotten her long ago in my heart, and in this moment, appreciated her for admitting the error of her ways and apologizing.

There was also a part of me that believed her bullying had led to my success today. I hadn't wanted to let the bullies win over me, and the only way they would was if I let their negativity defeat me and keep me from progressing forward. I was determined to do better, make something of myself, and have them all become distant memories.

I was so glad that I had kept my head raised high and focused on my goals, so that she and everyone could see that anyone can rise above the hurtful comments and the pain of the past.

If you are facing a painful situation, remember: Years down the road, as long as you stay focused on who you are and who you want to become, you might receive a message like this. And even if you don't, you can feel strong knowing that you didn't let it slow you down or hold you back. You will be yet one more example that no one can drag us down, and that it is so much better to rise up together.

TIFFANY'S TOP TEN TIPS FOR GETTING UP WHEN YOU'VE BEEN KNOCKED DOWN

1. **Visualize the future.** When someone puts you down, imagine if years from now you're telling the story of your career just like I am, and this is the story's turning point. What would come next? Do what it takes to make that happen.

2. **Be better.** Do one thing to help ensure that what happened to you won't happen to others, even if it's just smiling at someone new in the hallway. You can be better than the bullies.

3. **Remember, it's not personal.** Chances are, the person targeting you has bullied other people. Even if they're hating on specific qualities of yours, the opposite of what they're saying may be true. (Despite what was in that burn book, my hair looked great! It had always been the physical trait that others complimented then and even now.) People attack things they're jealous of. And if what they're saying is true, it may actually be a good thing. (My nerdiness has served me quite well!)

4. **Feel your feelings.** It's totally normal and okay to feel insecure, sad, or scared when you're the victim of bullying. Crying is healthy. If you're having trouble handling these emotions or you think sharing them would help, talk to someone you trust. There's no shame.

5. **Turn your pain into something beautiful.** You don't have to turn it into a platform like I did, but maybe you can turn it into a drawing, a poem, or a superintense workout. Use your emotions to fuel you forward.

6. **Prove your critics wrong.** Even if what was said about you is totally untrue, you can use these words as fuel for self-improvement by making them even *less* true. If they say you're not smart, channel your anger to do even better in school. If they say you're socially awkward, be extra friendly. Or if what they're saying is actually a strength, own it. If they say you're weird, show off your uniqueness (or go listen to the song "This Is Me" from the movie *The Greatest Showman*. Trust me—you'll feel less alone). By owning your uniqueness, you'll inspire others to do the same, and the haters' voices will fade into the background.

7. **Ask for help.** Bullies will try to make you feel like something's wrong with you, but remember, they're the ones who did something wrong. Tell a parent, a teacher, or another trusted adult. You deserve them on your side. Or if you just need a listening ear, talk

to a friend or classmate who you know will be supportive. If you'd prefer to ask for help anonymously, you can reach out on Mogul!

8. **Help other victims.** If you don't feel comfortable saying something in the moment, reach out to them afterward to see if they're okay. That way, you'll both have an ally.

9. **Kill them with kindness.** People bully others because they don't like themselves. So instead of trying to get back at your bullies, feel bad for them. When you can't avoid them, be civil to them. They may just come to realize that they can take the high road, too.

10. **Carry that kindness everywhere you go.** Finding it in your heart to be nice to everyone, even those who don't show you the same courtesy, can be inspiring. The more you kill with kindness, the better you'll feel about yourself. So take your newfound courage everywhere you go and, with each action, let the bullies know: They don't define you, and they never will.

JENNA USHKOWITZ

ACTRESS, SINGER, AND STAR OF *GLEE*

Jenny Anderson

JENNA USHKOWITZ

Through the many moments of my career, one of the highlights was being a part of a television show that entered people's living rooms every week and allowed them to see firsthand that being different can be a strength, that being yourself is always the right choice, and that if you look hard enough, you can find people who will accept you exactly as you are.

I've always been someone who has been known for being different. I didn't necessarily *ask* to be different, but I was the girl in school who modeled, who was in commercials, and who was on Broadway at a very young age. I never fit in doing extracurricular activities like cheerleading, or hanging out with friends after school.

If you stand out, you may become a target, but that's way better than forcing yourself to dim your own light. There were certainly times in my life where I haven't felt accepted, where I was made fun of for more than one reason, but I would try to never let it get me down. I *chose* positivity then, and I still do. I know that "different" is what makes me special, and try to remind myself that I'm doing work that is bigger than just myself. Here's to the end of trying to please others.

I now understand the strength of my inner confidence, and that being myself is enough—it's what allows me to move past the haters without a second thought. Sure, some days are harder than others, but we have to love ourselves first and foremost. Only then can we share that love with others. When you love yourself, there is no space for negativity, and that is when you understand that love is all you need.

If we can celebrate individuality and diversity, if we can find joy in who we uniquely are, we can eradicate the kind of pain that comes from girl-to-girl bullying.

It's why I wrote my book, *Choosing Glee*, and why I had a podcast called *Infinite Positivities*—to shine a light on others who have successfully found happiness within, and to learn how they work on themselves every day. **There is no reason to spread hate when we can spread light, joy, and love.** ▤

CHAPTER SEVEN
GIVING LEADS TO GETTING

If you ever start to feel discouraged, like all your hard work is for nothing, let me share a secret. The only time your hard work adds up to nothing is if you are working solely for your own benefit and you are concentrating on what *you* can get. But if you are focused on others and what you can offer them, your work is *always* worthwhile.

The reason that I've been able to push further and higher and longer and faster is because I've focused on what my hard work could provide to other people. Doing so has given me more than I ever could have imagined.

We all have something that gets us fired up. Something we're desperate to change, even if that means leaving our comfort zone. It's that passion that will develop our skills and stretch our limits the most. Because when we care about something larger than ourselves, we'll go to lengths we never thought possible. It doesn't have to be a lofty goal. The important thing is to think outside of your own wants and needs.

If you're working toward only your own goals, you'll eventually get tired. Your heart won't be in it. But if you give your heart and soul to something or someone else—a cause, a project, something greater than yourself—you will not be disappointed. No matter how much you give, you will always get something even greater in return.

It is true. Call it the path of reciprocity, the law of attraction, the power of hard work, whatever you want, but I know that if you give, you get. My life is living proof.

THE POWER OF ONE PERSON

One of the first times I experienced how much power we have as individuals to create change was during my sophomore year of high school. It was winter, and I remember bundling myself up in a puffy blue jacket to steel myself against what felt like frigid temperatures (though I'm sure it was probably

TALKING ABOUT MY TIME IN TEXAS WITH LO BOSWORTH OF MTV'S LAGUNA BEACH (SECOND FROM THE RIGHT) AND FRIENDS.

no colder than 45 degrees! It was Texas, after all). And as I rushed to get from the car to the warm halls of the high school, I remembered something I had been watching on the news the night before, about struggles in Afghanistan due to wintertime conditions. I remembered the faces of children shivering in what I'm sure were *actual* freezing temperatures. So as I walked into the bustling, cozy halls of my high school, I felt so blessed to have a warm jacket and a heated school. And I decided that I wanted to do something to help those Afghan children.

After a few hours researching online that evening, I had found an organization that was spearheading a clothing drive, and I vowed that I would collect donations from our school to contribute. By the next day, I had talked to administrators and gotten permission to put up a table outside the cafeteria and some signage to spread the word. I knew this location would provide the most foot traffic, and I would be able to talk to people when they weren't rushing off to class but had a few minutes to hear what I had to say. Each day at lunchtime, I would approach my classmates and talk to them about what I was doing. I quickly developed a kind of script. First, I would talk about why this was important to me, then I would discuss why this was important to them, and then we would discuss why this was important to the world. (This is still the rough script I use anytime I am pitching someone, whether it is with an investor, an advisor, or a potential client!) Soon, I had recruited some of my girlfriends to help me at lunch.

After a couple of weeks, I realized that I had saturated this market and it was time to expand. I began to talk to kids that I met at my SAT prep class, who attended different high schools. I knew if I could onboard additional representatives across these schools, we could have even broader reach.

One month later, we had collected 981 pieces of clothing to send to Afghanistan.

While I loved the feeling of knowing that the clothes we gathered helped children stay warm that winter, what that experience granted me was even greater than the feeling of having done something positive in the world. It gave me the confidence to realize that I could see a problem and do my small part to help. It taught me that I had agency. I had created an initiative at my school, and it brought so much good. I became addicted to that feeling.

It doesn't matter how old you are; you can begin to impact the world right now. Today, we are seeing this through the survivors of the Parkland shooting. High school students are frustrated by politicians' inability to act, and are creating their own initiatives, marches, and organizations to demand change. They are taking their anger and pain, and channeling it into the most important kind of action there is: the desire to make things better for the generations to come.

ENGAGE WITH THE WORLD AROUND YOU

As I mentioned before, one of the first ways I pulled myself out of my sheltered cocoon during college was by joining the

YOUR GET-INSPIRED VIEWING LIST

I first became aware of the plight of the Afghan people and their struggles with brutal winter conditions when I was watching the national news. When we witness problems, whether firsthand or through the media, our eyes are opened to other worldviews and experiences across the globe. We are also empowered to do something about them. One of the most effective ways to learn about important issues is through documentaries. Below are a few documentaries that not only educate but also helped to enact real change.

- *Child 31*: I was brought in to help produce this short documentary, and it continues to be one of my favorite examples of how much one person can achieve when they identify a problem, propose a solution, and do everything they can to see it through. The film follows Magnus MacFarlane-Barrow, founder of Mary's Meals, and how he is addressing two dire problems, starvation and lack of education for children, through one simple solution: one free meal at school per day in countries with the greatest need. Many children do not have enough to eat at home. Mary's Meals provides essential nutrition while also giving children a reason to go to school every day. Even if their only reason is to receive that food, they inadvertently are also receiving something just as important: education. Today, Mary's Meals serves more than one million meals per day.

- **Blackfish:** This revolutionary documentary released in 2013 examined the life of a killer whale at SeaWorld named Tilikum and the devastating effects of keeping a naturally predatory animal in captivity. The film was widely celebrated, and led to real change. When SeaWorld's profits declined significantly after the release, the company changed its breeding policies and shows. In fact, in 2016, SeaWorld made a statement promising that it would eventually stop featuring killer whales in shows at its water parks.

- **He Named Me Malala:** This documentary follows the remarkable life of Malala Yousafzai, the Pakistani girl who was shot in the face by the Taliban on her way home from school. The Taliban had recently declared that girls were no longer allowed to pursue education, and wanted to make an example of her. Malala miraculously survived and has committed her life to helping girls get access to the education they deserve, no matter where they live.

- **Catfish:** In 2010, when the world of social media was still a largely unexplored frontier, three filmmakers examined what can happen when you befriend someone online who turns out to be not who they claim to be. This was an entirely new phenomenon at the time, and the filmmakers turned it into a long-running television show on MTV once they realized how widespread this problem was. They coined the term *catfish*, and being *catfished*, and it is a phenomenon now well understood. But until this documentary, no one knew how careful we needed to be with our identities on the internet. It opened people's eyes to how they could be completely fooled, and thus served an important purpose in addressing a problem most people didn't even realize existed.

Asian American Students Association as its webmaster my sophomore year. And it was at one of the group's meetings that I got the nudge to put myself out there in an even bigger way.

The *Yale Herald* had run a cartoon that was, in short, racist toward Asian Americans. The newspaper had a great reputation on campus, and our group had a hard time accepting that it would have run something so offensive on purpose. Our guess was that the staff didn't realize it was offensive. Which meant that the *Herald* likely didn't have a diverse staff.

This is one of the reasons that diversity matters so greatly in our world today. People with different viewpoints and backgrounds have a full spectrum of experiences, leading to the creation of better content, a wider reach, and a more equal perspective.

Though I didn't say much at the AASA meeting, I knew that I had to do something about this problem. I was going to offer to join the staff of the *Herald* so that nothing like this would happen again.

The fact that I was focused on protecting others from a hurtful experience was the key to overcoming my insecurity. I didn't feel qualified to join the paper, but I knew someone had to in order to diversify the staff. Since nobody else stepped up, I was willing to leave my comfort zone and do it myself.

When I met with the publisher of

How can I find a way to get involved?

the *Herald*, I realized how small the staff was. There were really just two people running the entire thing, and the newspaper was close to bankruptcy.

I worked at the paper for the next two years, starting as a financial analyst and eventually being promoted to publisher. It was one of the most rewarding experiences of my college career.

Now, this meeting where we discussed the cartoon was just a simple meeting, like many others before and after it. But because I was paying attention and I asked myself what I could do about the issue, I created a path that ultimately led to a job that I loved and that taught me more than I could have imagined. Every day, there are small moments that can turn into pivot points if you take the time to notice them, whether you are in the classroom, at an after-school activity, or at an event. Always be asking: *How can I engage with the world around me in a new way? How can I find a way to get involved?* In our busy everyday lives, we can sometimes stay focused on our own problems, or solely on how something affects us. But the key to creating impact and finding opportunities to grow and learn and change is to open your eyes and look outside yourself. Engage with the world around you and identify problems that need to be solved. Don't wait for others to solve them. Solve them yourself. And then you'll see a path open up before you—the path of service, significance, and success.

ALWAYS BE KIND AND GENEROUS

If you approach a situation with the intent to give or help out in any way, you often end up being the one who receives. It is called the path of reciprocity. When you are good to people, they in turn will be good to you. When you offer to help with something out of unselfish ambitions, you will find yourself rewarded in return and then some.

While I was working at CBS, I befriended a guy named Alex who had started a media company. I knew that

USE YOUR ANGER
AS A CATALYST

What issues do you find yourself getting the most worked up about? What pain do you see in the world that you cannot turn away from? Use the anger you feel as fuel to begin to address the needs you see in front of you. Then ask yourself these questions:

What are some organizations that address this problem that I could volunteer for?

Is there someone who works in this space whom I could reach out to? You could ask for a phone call or an in-person meeting about what they are doing and how you could support them.

How can I make it personal? Find a photo or image that reminds you of a need you've identified, and post it somewhere you'll see it every day so that you will be regularly reminded of how you are invited to be a force of good in this world.

No one can change the entire world, but we can each do our own part to address one need. And these individual small efforts can add up to something amazing.

his business would greatly benefit by securing CBS as a client, so I happily provided an introduction. A few short months later, when I launched Mogul, he sent out an email to every single one of his advisors suggesting that they meet with me and not miss the chance to invest in my company.

One of those advisors was the cofounder of Match.com, and he became one of Mogul's first investors and advisors.

I didn't help Alex in hopes that he would one day help me. But I've seen time and again that when you stay focused on others and how you can help and support them, they do it in turn. You create a chain of love and support that allows everyone to reach their goals so much faster, together.

So I invite you to channel your energy not on what you can get from experiences, friendships, or opportunities, but on what you can give. Ask: *How could I step in and contribute? How could I make someone's life easier? Is there anything I could do to encourage, uplift, or make that person smile?*

They may be very small things! But putting positivity, kindness, and love out into the world, in big ways and small, truly adds up.

STAY TRUE TO YOURSELF AND YOUR PURPOSE

Obviously, being kind and generous is something I think the entire world could benefit from, and I've seen it pay off in my life more times than I can count. But I've also striven to find a purpose in everything I do, outside of just being kind. If you figure out what *you* are meant to do in the world, whenever the work gets hard you just return to the why, and it reenergizes you, refocuses you, and reorients you toward what really matters. When you stay focused on the big *why* of what you are working toward, you'll go to lengths you never thought possible. If you are only working for yourself, to get fame or more followers, to become the most popular, to get recognition from others, you'll eventually get tired. You won't have enough fuel.

But if you find a bigger goal, it will keep you going and push you further and higher than you ever imagined. You have to know why you are doing it. I know that was what kept me going during those exhausting days launching Mogul, when I was barely sleeping and the company existed only in my bedroom. I kept thinking of the hundreds of girls who had reached out to me for advice. They were my why. My family was also my why, with their examples of always extending a helping hand to others. Around my room, I posted the emails of thanks that I received from those young girls, along with a photo of my family, so that I had visual reminders all day long of why I was toiling so hard, of why I was pushing myself to do more and work harder. Seeing them reenergized me whenever I felt fatigue creeping in.

Not every moment of our lives is filled with purpose. We don't always feel the impact that we are having. There will be times in your life where you are questioning whether what you are doing is making any kind of difference, when you are anxious to get to those impactful moments when you know you are changing the world. There will be times when you have to be patient and know that though your goal *will* be realized, it sometimes takes longer than you think.

I had always dreamed of someday working at the United Nations, or at least having the kind of global impact the UN provides. The UN was enacting the kind of powerful change I wanted to accomplish. It was on the front lines of hope, providing help, aid, support, and

much-needed resources to the world.

When I was working in finance right after college, I was struggling with the day-to-day grind. It didn't feel like I was "doing" anything to contribute to the big picture, for the organization and for the world. One day, I found myself surfing through the UN website, and I saw an application for an internship. I filled it out and submitted it, and a few months later, I received a letter notifying me of my acceptance.

I sat there staring at the note from an organization that I had always wanted to work for. And I was tempted to turn in my notice and take this unpaid internship. I just wanted to feel like I was making a difference in the world! Wasn't this what I had gone to college for? So that I could be of service in the world?

I called my dad and told him about my struggle. My dad was kind and supportive; he understood my frustration and where I was coming from. But he said if I could see this analyst position through, go to business school, and build the company that I'd long dreamed of, that one day the UN would be inviting me to join it as an honored guest.

I remember that conversation like it was yesterday. It was such good advice. Sometimes along the path to where we want to go, we feel stuck in the mud, like we aren't getting there fast enough, that the work we are putting in isn't exacting any change, that we aren't making a difference, that we need to change course or do something else.

Sometimes, we need to be reminded to be patient. To stay focused on our end goal. To keep putting one foot in front of the other. Because we will get there. And it will be greater than we could have ever imagined.

Sure enough, five years later I was standing in front of the UN, giving a speech about Mogul's impact on our one-year anniversary. It was a pinch-me moment, where I couldn't help but remember my father's words of encouragement. He was right. So very right.

I'm not sure what your goals are. Some goals we set are finite, and we can accomplish them in a matter of months. Some goals are immense, and they will take years. Set both kinds of goals for yourself, and understand the difference. Remember that you can't always reach them overnight. Every day, as long as you stay focused on a goal, you are getting closer.

Set minigoals on the path to a long-term one so that you will have moments of celebration. Make a checklist of skills you need to acquire, and cross them off as you master each one. Make notes of people you want to reach out to and, again, cross them off once you've touched base. All forward movement is getting you closer. Stay focused on your why, which will allow you to stay fueled, and nothing can stop you.

stay focused on your why

YOUR GET-STARTED GUIDE
TO GET WHAT
YOU GIVE

There are so many ways to volunteer your time, pledge a commitment, and spread positivity and hope. Here are a few suggestions to get you started:

Try to say yes when someone asks you to do something. Okay, I know these days you often get the opposite advice: *Learn to say no! Don't spread yourself too thin!* But I think you'll see in this book that I often try to say yes. Not just for the chance to try something new or for another learning opportunity but because the more you give of yourself, of your time, of your resources, the more you'll receive in return.

Make a pledge to address a need that makes you deeply sad. Whether you are a person who cannot turn away from someone asking for money on the street, or whether you find yourself crying whenever you see those postings about a poor sea turtle impaled by straws in the ocean, take those moments of pain and turn them into purpose. Do a drive at your school for food to distribute to homeless people, or a clothing drive for winter coats during cold seasons. Reach out to an organization that helps educate people about the destructiveness of plastic straws and go to a few local businesses to see if you can post signage asking that customers think twice about using them. Your efforts don't have to take a lot of time, but it is a way for you to do something, anything, about a problem you see. This empowers you to do more and take on more, and you'll meet others who feel just as passionately as you do.

> **On the weekends, instead of going to the mall with your friends, invite them to join you in volunteering.** It could be at a local animal shelter, homeless shelter, pediatric hospital, or library. It is a great way to spend time together while also bringing positivity into the world.

Since I've launched Mogul, I remember my why every single day. Touching base daily with Mogul's mission throughout the company's growth has allowed me to stay calm and confident, even during difficult times. My goal was never about making a lot of money, though I know that the more profit we earned, the more we could give back. We are a social enterprise—a company focused on earning money so that we can then distribute it to worthy organizations, a company focused first and foremost on our community and how we might better serve them.

That first time I spoke at the UN was just the beginning. Two and a half years after that speech, Mogul officially partnered with UN Women, a branch of the UN focused on gender equality,

to offer free access to Mogul Learning courses to women in need across the globe. For every dollar that Mogul earns, there is one more woman who is granted access to life-changing resources and information.

In my wildest dreams, I might have imagined Mogul partnering with the UN, but those dreams would have been just that—wild. Unattainable. But sure enough, by our staying focused on what Mogul could provide to women, the UN came to us. They recognized the good we were doing, and therefore invited us to partner. It was honestly one of the highlights of my life.

I guess you could say Mogul is just one more case study proving that you truly do get what you give.

mogul mentor

ARIANNA HUFFINGTON
COFOUNDER OF *THE HUFFINGTON POST*
AND THRIVE GLOBAL

In April of 2007, I was taking my daughter around to look at prospective colleges. The ground rules we'd agreed on—or, more accurately, that my daughter demanded—were that during the trip I would not be on my phone. But that didn't mean I would stop working. My partners and I had founded the *Huffington Post* just two years earlier, and we were growing at an incredible pace. Surely the reason for the success, or so I told myself, was that I was working eighteen hours a day, seven days a week. Of course, I couldn't take five days off (sacrilege!). I was indispensable.

So each night after dinner, in some sort of role reversal, Christina would do the responsible thing and go to sleep while I acted the part of the sneaky teenager and stayed up late. After she'd fallen asleep, I'd fire up the computers

ARIANNA HUFFINGTON

and the (yes) BlackBerrys, responding to all the "urgent" emails and generally attempting to squeeze a full day's work into what should have been my sleep time.

When the trip was over, I didn't fly straight home. Instead, I flew first to

Portland for a speaking engagement, and then on to LA that night. After getting home very late, I was up again four hours later for an interview—one that I still have no idea why I said yes to. But there is that level of tiredness where you don't actually even notice you're tired anymore—like being drunk. And once I got to my office after the interview, my body just couldn't take it anymore, and down I went, coming back to consciousness in a pool of blood and having broken my cheekbone on the way down.

Afterward, as I went from doctor to doctor to find out if there was any underlying medical problem, I had a chance to ask myself a lot of questions about the kind of life I was living, like, Was this the life I wanted? Is this really what success looks like? And what I found out was that what I was suffering from was an acute case of burnout. So I made changes to my life as I learned more and more about the connection between well-being and productivity. That led to writing my books *Thrive* and *The Sleep Revolution*.

As I went around the world speaking about the issues of stress and burnout, I saw how deeply people want to change their lives. So I wanted to go beyond just speaking out and raising awareness—I felt the need to turn this passion into something real and tangible that would begin to help people to actually change their daily lives. It was a call to action I just couldn't ignore, and so I founded Thrive Global.

I've always loved helping people engage and connect (I'm Greek; that's what we do—lure you to the table to eat and talk). That's what HuffPost was and that's what Thrive Global is now—helping people unplug and recharge so they can connect with others and with themselves. **This mission—changing the way we work and live so we can all thrive—is something I'm deeply passionate about, and makes it a joy to come to work every day.** ▦

CHAPTER EIGHT
PROFESSIONAL FANGIRLING

We all have those people that we look up to, respect, and dream of one day meeting. Whether it is your favorite singer, a writer who you love, an activist who motivates you, or a politician you see making important changes in policy, it is essential to have people who inspire you. Role models give us something to strive for and the opportunity to dream big. One of the reasons that I built Mogul was to ensure that girls around the world have access to role models, no matter how their society tries to limit women. I knew how powerful it was for me to have someone to look up to, to show me what was possible.

But here's where you have a chance to change your life. What if you reached out to the very people you admire, and asked if you could get involved in what they are doing?

That's right. In this chapter, I'm going to show you the art of becoming a professional fangirl. This does not involve cyberstalking or obsessing over

someone. It simply means taking active steps to reach out to people you respect. It means taking a chance, offering to help, and seeing what doors open to you.

it never hurts to ask.

You've heard the phrase *It never hurts to ask.* I'm here to tell you that not only does it not hurt, but asking is one of the most powerful things you can do.

REACH OUT TO YOUR ROLE MODELS

The first time I attempted this tactic, I was in high school. I emailed a fan letter to Kari Kimmel, a singer-songwriter whose songs have been featured in hundreds of films and television shows, such as *The Office* and *Keeping Up with the Kardashians*. A popular *American*

© Mark Meyer

I GOT MORE THAN A SIGNED PHOTO FROM SONGWRITER KARI KIMMEL—I GOT MY FIRST INTERNSHIP!

Idol contestant named Kimberley Locke had selected Kari's song "I Could" as one of her first singles when she landed a record deal, and upon listening to it on the radio for the first time, I was hooked. I found Kari's site and sent a note to the email listed, letting her know how much the song lyrics had

meant to me and asking her if there might be ways in which I could spread the word about her work.

At first, I was scared that my absolute adoration of her artistry would make me come off as young and silly. Instead, my enthusiasm made her feel appreciated. I was shocked when she responded with a kind note and shared how much it meant to her. As we continued to correspond via email, I decided to take things a step further and ask again, this time more specifically: *Could I help you in any way whatsoever? Is there anything you may need at the moment that I could support you on?* I wasn't entirely sure what I could do, but I knew I loved her work, creativity, and drive. I wanted to be a part of it, even from my bedroom in Plano, Texas.

Just a few days later, she responded with an offer for me to begin to manage her website and fan letters—years before I'd ever received fan letters of my own.

This was essentially my first internship. No, I didn't get paid for it. I didn't care about the money! I knew it was an opportunity to learn through the experience.

I worked night and day, answering and organizing each fan letter immediately, displaying attentiveness, dedication, and enthusiasm. Kari was greatly impressed. She respected my work ethic, and subsequently gave me more responsibility. From this experience, I developed early skill sets in website development, branding, and marketing, as well as customer support. My offer to volunteer turned into a collaboration that turned into a long-term partnership. And we are still friends to this day.

So, who do you look up to? Who is working in the industry you aspire to join? Gather the courage to reach out. Ask if there is a way for you to get involved in what they are doing. What could you take off their plate to make their lives easier?

When you get your foot in the door by helping out with something (anything!), it allows you to begin to build a relationship—with that person, their staff, and their organization. By helping them, you inevitably open yourself up to an amazing learning opportunity.

This is an approach that has been incredibly helpful for me throughout my career as I've sought out mentors and advisors. I have never been focused on what *they* could give *me*. Instead, I approached these people with an attitude of generosity. Was there anything I could do to help them? When you stay focused on what *you* can bring of value, you'll find that people are more likely to say yes to your offer. And that will become your best way to learn.

And don't worry—you *do* have something of value to offer. Your value could be your skills as a calligrapher, and you could offer to help address invitations. Your skill set could be web design, and you could offer to work on their website or create ads for them. Your talent could be creative social media engagement, and you could help manage their social media presence.

But sometimes, just a willingness to step into any role is what is most needed. Offer your help broadly and see what happens.

YOUR EMAIL CHEAT SHEET

Think of ten different people you look up to and greatly respect. Politely request their email addresses by connecting with them through Mogul, or direct message them via a social media platform such as Instagram or Facebook. Remember to stay focused on your offer to help.

Here's a sample email template to use.

Dear X,

I'm currently a student at X. I've heard wonderful things about you and how you have been running X [describe something that shows how much you admire their work and that you are familiar with their career and achievements]. I am involved in the following activities and am striving to give back to my community through X.

I'd love to get together to discuss ways in which I might be able to support and collaborate on your current initiatives. Would it be possible to set up a phone call to discuss the various ways I might be able to assist? In particular, I've been working on my X skills for quite some time, so I would be thrilled to help with X.

I would so greatly appreciate if you were available on X, between X A.M. and X P.M., or X, between X A.M. and X P.M.

Thank you, and I look forward to hearing from you.
Me

If you don't hear anything back, don't get discouraged! Just wait a week or two and then gently follow up. Not everyone will respond. But if you reach out to ten people, maybe three people will reply to you. And if even one person agrees to a phone call, it can make all the difference.

Then write to ten more people, and ten more after that. Just one opportunity can set you up with contacts and experiences that will serve you for life.

say yes

USE YOUR CONNECTIONS

Another strategy you can use to connect with potential mentors is to look within your current circle of contacts to see if there is someone who can connect you personally to one of your idols. I call this a "warm connection" (as opposed to the dreaded "cold call"). In college, one of my best friends was Lizzi, and I knew that her father, Rob, worked in entertainment. After I graduated, I worked up the courage to ask Lizzi whether she would mind providing an introduction to her father and letting him know that I was looking for ways to get involved in the industry. She was thrilled to help, and before I knew it, he and I were connected via email. He told me that he was developing an off-off-Broadway musical called *Volleygirls*. Would I be interested in reading the script and sending some feedback?

I said yes, of course. I was thrilled! I was just out of college, looking for in-roads into the entertainment industry, and this was perfect. As soon as he sent it to me, I read through the entire script twice. By the end of the evening, I'd sent back detailed edits.

That relatively straightforward job—providing edits on the script—led to sitting in on an in-person read-through of the show, where I befriended another one of the producers, NBC TV star Monica Raymund (now one of our Mogul users). Rob had invited me to the read-through likely not expecting me to actually show up, given that there would be little for me to do other than just listen. But I did show up. And that showed my commitment.

Next, once the show went into previews, Rob asked me to be the check-in girl. I knew I was supposed to keep track of who attended, in the hopes that Rob might be able to secure their support for the show thereafter, and that doing this job well was incredibly important. So I showed up that first night with my laptop and an Excel spreadsheet, and I

CREATE
YOUR OWN
INTERNSHIP

If you think about it, this offer of "helping for free and learning through the process" is the basis for the entire internship industry. But you don't have to wait until summer or apply through a formal program. You have the tools to track people down and offer to help all on your own. You'll stand out from the crowd because of your initiative. And, believe me, when you start taking your future into your own hands instead of waiting around for the right opportunity to present itself, you'll feel incredibly empowered, like nothing can stop you.

List three people you want to reach out to and
circle whether they're cold calls or warm connections:

_____ (cold call or warm connection?)
_____ (cold call or warm connection?)
_____ (cold call or warm connection?)

Next to each name,
write down the date you reached out
so that you can remember
when to follow up.

more than checked people in—I created an entire database of potential partners for the show. When I sent that first file to Rob, he couldn't believe the level of detail and organization I had brought to the job. And just a few weeks later, he promoted me to general manager of the show.

I was in my early twenties and working two other jobs at the time, but it was such an incredible and unexpected honor to be named a general manager of a musical in New York City. It stemmed from a warm introduction through a good friend, but it would have stalled out if I hadn't overdelivered on every task I was given. I went above and beyond on every job Rob gave me so that he could see that I could handle more responsibility.

If you want to be a professional fangirl, you can't just admire. You've got to truly bring value to those people you end up working for.

I wish I could say that I achieved great success solely based on hard work and a lot of moxie. But I know firsthand how important finding the right people is for opening doors to opportunity. Once you find them, if you are good to them, kind to them, respectful, and hardworking, they will recommend you to others. This is another example of the path of reciprocity. So always be kind, generous, willing to help, and willing to go the extra mile.

FRIENDSHIP FIRST

Over the years, my approach as a fangirl has always been to remain focused not just on building a professional relationship with someone I admire but also on creating a true friendship. From the start, I always remember to be respectful, and share how and why I appreciate their work, but once we meet, I treat them as a friend. Okay, so maybe not always like my friends my own age. I never try to gossip about crushes or anything like that. But even now, I make sure to ask my mentors about themselves—about both their job and their life—in a warm, polite, and respectful way. My main goal is to get to know a person, not to "get" something from them. People feel the difference between digging for information and a genuine interest in who they are.

This approach is different from typical "networking," what many call meeting people in a certain industry just to find a connection that could lead to a job or promotion. While I'm all for staying connected and meeting new people, I've never liked the term *networking*, because of the suggestion it carries of being focused on getting something out of an interaction. I recommend building actual relationships with people who could become friends, collaborators, and partners. Networking can be perceived as cold, transactional, and short-term, whereas friendship is warm, focused on teamwork and support, and long-lasting.

Once I've made a connection with someone, I work to keep that relationship strong. And it has led to me working with many of the same people over and over throughout my career.

the time is now.

EMULATE—DON'T IMITATE

So have you identified someone you can reach out to yet? The time is now. Thanks to the power of the internet, it doesn't matter where you live. You can help anyone, anywhere, as long as you have a strong internet connection. But remember that you are looking to learn, not follow their footsteps exactly. Your path won't look just like theirs, nor should it! Don't try to be the next so-and-so. Try to be the first and only you. That uniqueness is what will allow you to find your place in the world.

Still, I know firsthand how connecting with the right mentors can really help you forge your own path. Your learning can start today. You can do work in the hours you have between school and bedtime, or on weekends. And here's another secret: If you find the right people to shadow, it never feels like work! It just feels like hanging out with incredibly cool people, doing amazing stuff, and developing a ton of new skills that you can apply to whatever it is you dream of doing.

MY TOP FIVE
FANGIRL MOMENTS

1

Emailing Kari Kimmel to see if there
was anything I could do to help her.

2

Overdelivering for Rob Ackerman
and his team on *Volleygirls*.

3

Reaching out to the cofounder of Match.com
to be our first investor in Mogul.

4

Approaching Anne Hidalgo, the first female mayor
of Paris, to be one of our first Mogul users.

5

Being asked to speak at the United Nations, an organization that
I had always admired and dreamed of working with one day. That
first talk led to future conversations, and eventually the chance to
officially collaborate with UN Women to bring educational
resources to girls in need across the globe.

FOCUS YOUR
FANGIRL

concentrate
✓ Concentrate on how you can help people,
not the other way around.

go beyond
✓ Always go above and beyond
what they ask of you.

respond
✓ Respond in a timely manner to
every request they make,
if even just to confirm that you received their note.

show respect
✓ Be respectful of their time.

be genuine
✓ Show genuine interest in them and their lives.

FRAN HAUSER

INVESTOR, FORMER PRESIDENT
OF DIGITAL AT TIME INC., AND AUTHOR
OF *THE MYTH OF THE NICE GIRL*

JUST ASK!

I've worked at a lot of exciting places and accomplished plenty of milestones throughout my career. But it wasn't until I began getting involved in early-stage investing in companies started by women that I truly felt like I had found my passion. I love being able to give these women a chance, and help them create the companies of their dreams. Now, I don't invest in women-led companies to be nice or simply because I believe we need more female representation (though I know we do). I do it because these entrepreneurs bring a new perspective, a deep understanding of market problems that are unique to women, and the passion, grit, and drive necessary to grow successful businesses.

Plus, did you know that tech start-

FRAN HAUSER

ups with female executives achieve a 35 percent higher return on investment? Investing in companies founded and led by women is a smart business decision.

While access to capital itself is a major roadblock for many women, it's not the only one. Young female entrepreneurs often don't have access to the networks their male counterparts do. Moreover, because there's a lack of female leadership in venture capitalism and at venture-backed companies, young women often don't have role models to look up to. A lack of mentorship and resources, as well as closed networks, means many women can't even get in the room to pitch their companies in the first place.

For these reasons, my focus is not only funding women but also advising them.

Mentorship is my way of paying it forward.

While there's a limit to how many dollars you can invest, there's no limit on the number of introductions you can make or how many young women you can inspire. Mentorship is my way of paying it forward.

Combined with my investments, it's how I'm working to close the gap in the venture capital and startup worlds.

And I'm not alone. More and more women and men are working to change the ratio, by advising young women, sharing stories, providing encouragement, and introducing these emerging leaders to the right people. We do it consciously. We do it regularly. We do it because we know it's making a difference.

So don't be afraid to reach out. Ask for a meeting, a relationship, an internship.

We are more than ready and willing to lend a hand to help you reach your goals.

We are looking for you, the leaders of the next generation. ⬓

PART THREE

Envision your future and make it happen.

CHAPTER NINE
DISCOVERING YOUR PASSIONS

Becoming a Girl Mogul is not about following someone else's path to success. It is about figuring out what you love to do and charting your own way forward. This section of the book is all about commitment: deciding what it is you want to do and then committing to accomplishing that goal. But it starts with identifying your passions and determining how you can incorporate them into what you commit your life to.

The earlier you can discover your passions, the better. I was lucky enough to set the blueprint for what I wanted to do with my life when I was relatively young. I knew I wanted to build my own company, and that I wanted that company to empower women. I didn't know exactly what that would look like, but I knew enough to know what skills I would need to develop. These skill sets became a kind of checklist of experiences that I needed to have under my belt so that when the time came, I would be ready to go out on my own.

So I invite you to use your passions to envision what your future could be, and then take the steps necessary to make it happen.

CAST YOUR NET WIDELY

My parents didn't have firm expectations for their children's future, or a trajectory that they wanted our lives to take. But that didn't mean they allowed us to sit at home all day. They were lovers of learning, and they instilled that value in me and my siblings. We were allowed to try anything we wanted, whether it was violin, soccer, art, or poetry. If we loved it, we were encouraged to become the best we could be at it. If we didn't enjoy it, we were allowed to let it go and find something else. My parents knew that when we found activities that we truly loved, that's when we would learn to excel at them. They taught me to recognize how powerful it can be to find something that you are

ATTENDING THE EMMYS FOR MY SIDE PROJECTS.

trying new things, in high school and beyond. In college, I did more than just pour myself into classes and socialize with friends. Not only was I webmaster of the Asian American Students Association, financial analyst and then publisher of a newspaper, and editor of a magazine, but I was also brought in to help produce a musical one of my friends had written. During the two years I worked at Credit Suisse, I was not just crunching numbers and learning as much as I could about the financial world but also reaching out to people in the entertainment industry, and eventually became the general manager of *Volleygirls*. During my two years in business school, while I focused on being prepared in class, and volunteered to organize my section retreat, I also served as the president of the Entertainment & Media Club and helped secure distributors for a film called *Girlfriend*. By the time I was at CBS, I was used to having two or three side projects that I would work on after hours. Soon I found myself working on the Beijing International Screenwriting

passionate about. Because when you love what you are doing, it doesn't feel like work.

Because of that lesson, I was always

Competition (which you'll read more about in a minute), collaborating with my brother and dad on a book, and teaching myself how to code.

See the pattern? It has served me very well to spread my efforts widely—not just to learn as much as I can and to refine what my passions truly are but also to make as many connections as I can. Each time I tried something new, I met potential friends and collaborators, who would in turn bring new adventures. It was like a never-ending cycle of fun, friends, and fantastic learning opportunities.

I know it sounds like I work from morning to night and don't have much time for a social life. But whenever I'm faced with a new opportunity, my motto is *What can I learn from this?* If there is something new to learn, an unacquired skill to add to my arsenal, I'll often say yes. To find your passions, you've got to try a lot of different things. Plus, it's fun!

Now, some people know their exact passion and pour themselves fully into it in order to excel. Think of professional athletes or musicians or artists. They aren't spreading themselves out widely to develop a lot of skills. They know what they are good at and focus on that one thing. But if you want to be an entrepreneur or run a business, or if you aren't sure what your passions truly are, pursuing a wide and varied path will serve you well.

Not everything I was doing was my actual passion. But learning something new was always worth it for me, even if the work itself wasn't that rewarding. And each experience added to my ability to refine what it was I was truly meant to do.

DETERMINING YOUR PASSION AS THE PATH TO YOUR CAREER

Even though I didn't know exactly what career path I might take, I did have a few themes that kept popping up in all of my projects. Storytelling. Empowering women. And highlighting diverse and/or underrepresented voices.

In fact, when I was still in high school, I came up with the idea of

DON'T OBSESS OVER WHAT YOU ARE GOING TO "DO" WHEN YOU GROW UP

I can't tell you how many people I see stuck because they think they need to know exactly what they want to do with their lives. When I was in high school, I didn't know exactly what I was going to do, either, but I had a broad idea of what I was interested in. That broad idea allowed me to pursue different opportunities that would allow me to refine that concept.

In fact, college can be a great opportunity to take classes on varied subjects. I know you may feel pressured to decide your major early on, but if you have the chance to attend a liberal arts college that values your taking courses in various disciplines, you have a chance to be exposed to new things.

Think of three things you might enjoy doing as a career, and ask yourself what you'd need to do *now* in order to be doing at least one of those things in five years. For example, if you want to be an artist, could you volunteer at a local gallery? If you think you might want to work in the technology sector, could you sign up for a camp that teaches you to code? If you're interested in politics, could you find an internship with a local campaign? The more of these first steps you take, the sooner you'll realize whether you want to walk farther down each path.

POTENTIAL CAREER #1:

_____

POTENTIAL FIRST STEP TO TAKE TODAY:

_____

_____

POTENTIAL CAREER #2:

_____

POTENTIAL FIRST STEP TO TAKE TODAY:

_____

_____

POTENTIAL CAREER #3:

_____

POTENTIAL FIRST STEP TO TAKE TODAY:

_____

_____

creating a website for teens. The site I envisioned would be the opposite of a burn book. It would be a place of support, love, and acceptance. A place

A place of support, love, and acceptance.

that gave every girl a voice: nerdy girls, artsy girls, girls of all sizes, girls of all races, girls of all abilities. I struggled with the fact that I didn't see anyone who looked like me reflected in any of the media around me. And I began to wonder: *If the media was always going to exclude me, maybe I could create my own platform that would include everyone.*

This idea of diversity, of inclusion, of finding a place where I could see myself reflected, was a powerful dream of mine. As I began to think more about this website, I took the time to sketch in a notebook what it might look like. I imagined that it would break down important areas of our lives: school, beauty, relationships, friendship, college applications. I even sketched out what the home page might look like: a grid of nine boxes with different subjects that people could click on. The boxes were one of three colors: orange, coral, or yellow. The font would be black.

I didn't realize it at the time, but this was the first version of Mogul. And that is the exact color palette of Mogul today.

So don't be afraid to be creative and imaginative about where your life might go. Those very dreams might just lead you to the next project to pursue, which will further refine your passions. The silly brainstorm of an idea that you began to conceptualize at age sixteen could be the very thing that you will build your career on at age twenty-seven.

Again, I didn't know at the time exactly what I wanted the website to be, and I wasn't entirely sure where I was heading. But the overall concept, and what it could bring to the world, became a guiding force for me. When I applied to colleges, I mentioned this passion that I had in my application essays: I said I dreamed to create a company for women that would allow them to come together and support one another, and to provide a portal of information and ideas specifically geared toward this audience. I explained that I wanted women to be able to share their own stories, to empower themselves and others. Though the college application process can be exhausting, writing my essays allowed me to refine what I wanted to do and the story line I was creating for my life. It made me crystalize where I hoped to one day be.

Whether you've already faced the college admissions process or are just beginning to think about where your future is headed, it is always helpful to check back in with yourself and ensure that you are headed down a path that will lead to fulfillment and not just a salary, job security, or prestige. What are causes that you find yourself volunteering for again and again? What are the classes that you cannot wait to get to? What activities do you find yourself completely immersed in, where before you know it hours have passed and you didn't even realize it?

Determining your passions comes from engagement with the world around you. It comes from trying new things, finding opportunities to get involved, and refining from there what you love the most.

TAKE IT ONE STEP AT A TIME

It's not like I woke up one day and was all of a sudden ready to start my own company from scratch. I know that Mogul's success came from the fact that I had taken enough steps before creating it. I had determined my passions and worked to build up my skill sets, so that when that day came, I would be ready. I wouldn't crumble under the weight of

timeline

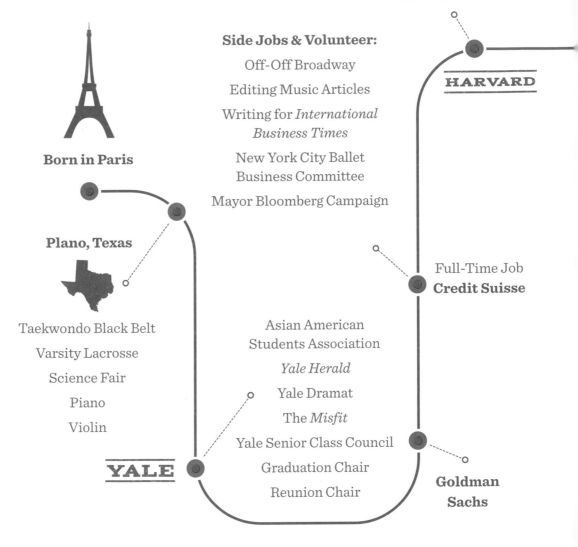

Born in Paris

Plano, Texas

Taekwondo Black Belt

Varsity Lacrosse

Science Fair

Piano

Violin

Harvard Business School

President of Entertainment
& Media Club

HARVARD

Side Jobs & Volunteer:

Off-Off Broadway

Editing Music Articles

Writing for *International
Business Times*

New York City Ballet
Business Committee

Mayor Bloomberg Campaign

Full-Time Job
Credit Suisse

Asian American
Students Association

Yale Herald

Yale Dramat

The *Misfit*

Yale Senior Class Council

Graduation Chair

Reunion Chair

YALE

**Goldman
Sachs**

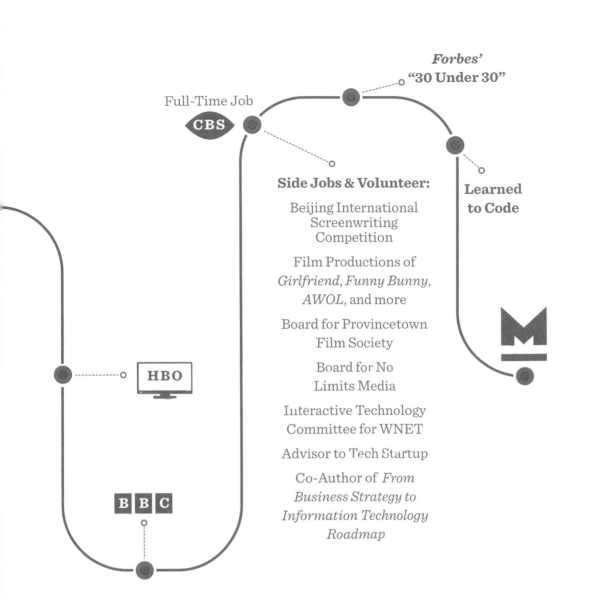

Forbes' "30 Under 30"

Full-Time Job

CBS

Side Jobs & Volunteer:

Beijing International Screenwriting Competition

Film Productions of *Girlfriend, Funny Bunny, AWOL,* and more

Board for Provincetown Film Society

Board for No Limits Media

Interactive Technology Committee for WNET

Advisor to Tech Startup

Co-Author of *From Business Strategy to Information Technology Roadmap*

Learned to Code

HBO

B B C

responsibility and the pressure of expectations. I would stand firm, knowing that I could handle it.

Looking back on the years leading up to Mogul's creation, I see a pattern of taking one step after another to gain the pertinent skill sets that would equip me to launch the site. I knew running a company successfully meant gaining expertise in its various departments: marketing, technology, operations, strategy and business development, content creation, and finance. I would often develop one skill set in my nine-to-five job, and additional skill sets in my side hustles. At Credit Suisse, I honed my financial skill set, while on the side I began to write for the *International Business Times* and joined the New York City Ballet business committee to learn more about fundraising. Once I started working at CBS, my role as Director of business development allowed me to create big-picture strategies to help a company broaden its reach and monetize all of its assets. Producing films developed my expertise in pitching (for investors or distributors),

while simultaneously teaching me what it took to create viral content.

One of the last side projects I took on before I launched Mogul was the Beijing International Screenwriting Competition, a venture that I was involved with from the very beginning in every aspect. I partnered with a friend I'd met at Harvard to launch the entire endeavor, in partnership with a vice mayor of Beijing and the city's Cultural Assets Office. It would be a competition for aspiring screenwriters to get financing for their projects, as long as their film was centered around or based in Beijing. We hired a team that we trusted to help us run it, created the strategy for how we would reach the screenwriters who could enter the competition, formed the panel of judges, and finally, reached out to over four hundred media outlets to spread the word. Every part of the venture was a test of my skills.

Was I ready? Could I really take a project from start to finish and make it a success?

When we received nearly one thousand screenplay submissions, and ultimately put on a lavish awards reception in downtown LA, attended by the press, Hollywood luminaries, and political elites, I knew the answer was yes.

I know that being involved in that endeavor played a part in my being chosen for *Forbes'* "30 Under 30" list, which was the catalyst for me to finally begin building Mogul. Even more, my experience with the Beijing International Screenwriting Competition gave me the confidence to take that leap of faith, to teach myself to code, and to actually begin to build my own company.

I had taken this project and made it a huge success. When I started getting those emails from girls across the globe, it was like an invitation waiting for me to open it. I knew I was ready to say yes to this opportunity, an opportunity that I had been waiting for my entire life. I was ready to risk it all and create something of my own.

There is a reason why people say, "Follow your passions." Because they will lead you exactly where you are meant to go.

GIVE YOURSELF PERMISSION

Ultimately, even after you identify your passions and figure out what you truly want to do in this world, you still have to take one last step. You have to say yes to the invitation presented to you. You have to give yourself permission to pursue it. You have to tell yourself it is okay to do what it is that you truly love to do.

RECEIVING AN AWARD FOR MOGUL IN TIMES SQUARE.

Sometimes this can be the most challenging step. The world loves to shut down new ideas and crush optimistic spirits. The world wants us to stick to the predictable path, the comfortable, well-trodden one.

To be a girl Mogul, you've got to get uncomfortable.

It is scary to pursue your passions, especially if you desire to pursue an avenue that has often been the purview of men, like engineering, politics, or the military. But we need you to be willing to be a pioneer! So that those who come after you no longer feel like outsiders. When we work together to break down long-held assumptions about what women can and cannot do, we open up pathways for the generations to come.

Actor and director Greta Gerwig didn't think that being a director was a possibility until she started watching indie films in college and saw that *Beau Travail*, a film that helped her truly understand cinema, was directed by a woman, Claire Denis. She thought: *That's a job you can have?*

Her senior year, Greta was at the South by Southwest Film Festival when she saw a film directed by a woman who was her age. Again, she was confused, thinking: *Wait, are we allowed to do that? Who told her that she could?*

It took her another decade, and some not-too-subtle signs, before she gave herself permission to try directing.

She was leaving actor and director Miranda July's house one day when Miranda offered her a pair of shoes that didn't fit Miranda well. Greta accepted them graciously. A few months later, Rebecca Miller, who was directing Greta in *Maggie's Plan*, passed along a pair of her old shoes. At this point, Greta began to see the message. Two female directors in the course of two months had given her shoes to literally step into. What was she waiting for?

Greta's directorial debut, *Lady Bird*, premiered in 2017 and was nominated for five Oscars, including Best Director. She is just the fifth woman to have been nominated for that award . . . ever. But she hopes that public acceptance of her film and its many accolades will empower the next generation of women to realize that they can pursue this path from the start. They no longer have to wait for permission.

I recently read an interview in *Glamour* magazine with actress and producer Reese Witherspoon, a woman who is committed to bringing women's stories and voices to the forefront. She has long been inspired by Mindy Kaling, whom she befriended while filming *A Wrinkle in Time* (also directed by a woman, the brilliant Ava DuVernay). Mindy is a pioneer in her own right—a woman of color who wrote, produced, and starred in her own network sitcom. And Reese asked Mindy one day: "Don't you ever get exhausted by always having to create your own roles?" Mindy said, "Reese, I've never had anything that I didn't create for myself."

Pursuing your passions means giving yourself a pep talk every day to do something new, ambitious, and scary. It means creating the very opportunities that you desire. It means no longer waiting for permission, but granting it to yourself.

WHY NOT ME?

When I first dreamed about building Mogul, I knew that one of the biggest hurdles I would need to overcome was the fact that I didn't know how to build a website. But I knew that I could learn. Ultimately, I wanted to be involved in

WHAT DOES A PASSION LOOK LIKE?

Okay, passion can appear in a number of different ways. It can go back to a cause that you care deeply about, like we talked about in chapter 7. It can be a skill you have that either comes naturally, or that you love to do so much that you work your ass off to get good at it, like running, singing, photography, or art. It can be writing, or connecting with people online, helping people feel valued and listened to. You don't have to know exactly where your passion is leading you. You just have to listen within and notice what you enjoy. Follow that lead. Take one step toward pursuing that passion, and then the next, and then the next. You don't always know where it's leading—like a trail of bread crumbs. But if you are doing something you love, you are on the right path.

every step of building my own company. I didn't want to farm out anything to other experts. I wanted to become an expert myself.

The fact that I coded Mogul was often that final piece that allowed investors to see how committed I was to this company and that I was willing to do what it takes to make Mogul a huge success. That little extra bit of effort (okay, it was really three months of a lot of effort!) led to the ultimate success of my company.

As mentioned before, women notoriously think they need to be 100 percent qualified before they will try something or apply for a job. But the world needs us to step up and admit that we don't know everything but that we are more than willing and able to learn. We are seeing this happening in the surge of women running for office in response to the 2016 presidential election. Worried that causes that are important to women will continue to be neglected or that all the progress we have made will be repealed, women have stepped into the political arena in droves, despite their lack of experience. "I always thought this was for other people, and I was not qualified," said Chrissy Houlahan, a candidate for US Congress in a 2018 *Time* article by Charlotte Alter. "There was this wake-up call of why not me?"

Remember Mindy Kaling's book title?

Why not, indeed.

Your passions and your commitment to learn will take you everywhere you want to go. Give yourself permission to discover those passions, pursue those passions, and commit to those passions even if you don't 100 percent know what you are doing. You are brilliant and capable and will be able to learn as you go.

The world needs you to step up and say yes.

Everyone at Mogul is supporting you every step of the way.

MONIQUE COLEMAN
ACTRESS AND CEO OF
MOTIVATED PRODUCTIONS

Each of us is born with a unique set of talents, gifts, and natural abilities, but it's our passion that fuels our dreams and takes us to the next level. When we're feeling stuck, it's often because we are out of alignment with our true desires. Here are three reasons that I'm a champion of following your internal navigation and letting it take you to unimaginable places.

1. Your passion unlocks your purpose.

I used to dream of being an actress in Hollywood and making films that moved people to tears or laughter, or simply entertained them. But I've come to understand that what I really wanted deep down was to make a positive impact on the world. Acting is just one vehicle to do so. However, my passion for acting led me to *High School Musical*, which helped me uncover

MONIQUE COLEMAN

Wes Klain

my purpose—which is to empower and inspire young people (especially girls) to pursue their dreams and unleash their full potential. This took me to the United Nations, where I was named as a Youth Champion, and to the UN Foundation organization Girl Up, allowing me to travel to over forty countries advocating on behalf of youth. I would have never dreamed of these things specifically, but they were the result of following my passion.

2. Your passion sustains you.

Inevitably, we all face challenges in life and encounter moments where we want to throw in the towel. However, living from your deepest passions gives you new energy and the power to overcome the darkest moments. Roadblocks and obstacles arise so we can grow. Being practical will never get us as far as being passionate will. So, next time things get tough, take bigger risks, practice radical gratitude, and choose to do what lights you up. We only get one life, so we may as well make it the best we can!

3. Your passion elevates you.

I've found that since I've allowed passion to guide me, the opportunities that I'm met with are truer to *all* aspects of my life. When I started acting, I felt like I was missing something, which led me into philanthropy and advocacy. But when I was just speaking, or championing causes, I felt like I'd lost my fire. My artist soul was empty. For years, I sought balance, and I finally feel like I've found it. One of my recent projects is the exact intersection of purpose and passion! I played a guidance counselor, Katina Howard, in the third season of the AwesomenessTV show *Guidance*. I get to tackle issues like racism, slut-shaming, and bullying—all things I'm passionate about.

I hope my experience helps you to trust that your passion will guide you, elevate you, and sustain you. There is only one you on the planet, so when you activate the unique combination of who you really are and what you deeply want, you carve out your own lane. **You being you and following your heart will make the world better! Promise.** ▓

CHAPTER TEN
CRUSHING IT

Remember how I was the check-in girl at an off-off-Broadway musical, and I went above and beyond on every task given to me—until I was ultimately promoted to general manager of the show?

That was an example of a tool that I've used to get ahead in life over and over, and it always delivers. Crush it in everything you do, and you'll find yourself with more responsibility, more oversight, and more job offers than you could have ever imagined. When someone gives you a task, even a mundane one, don't do what's asked of you. Imagine what more you could do that might be helpful. Then do that. Then ask yourself again: *What else could I do?* Then do that. Over and over, again and again.

People are always looking for "hacks" to do better in school, work, or life. But there's always one obvious trick—it's just not one people like to hear. That trick is to work harder than the people around you. Crush it in every

avenue, and watch your dreams materialize in front of you.

OVERPREPARE AND OVERDELIVER

My first taste of what can happen when you overprepare and then overdeliver came when I finally earned that first 100% in math class after following Diane's example. It was truly a pivotal moment in my life: I experienced the sweetness of applying myself to a

Crush it in everything you do.

task and actually succeeding. At first, I thought that Diane was just smarter than me (and that might still be true!). But soon, I realized she especially excelled because she was willing to put in the work.

I then applied that willingness to work hard, that discipline, to tae kwon do and lacrosse, earning a black belt when I was sixteen and making the varsity lacrosse team when I was just a junior. I diligently applied myself to violin and piano, practicing over and over again, at home and at school, until I made first chair in the school orchestra and ranked among the top players in the city for both instruments.

But notice that it is a two-step process. You've got to overprepare before you can overdeliver. Overpreparing means hours of practice and extra studying. It means making that detailed schedule of your week so you can ensure that you complete everything on time. It means thinking through every possible scenario and identifying how you could address each one. It means creating an Excel spreadsheet when most people would use a piece of paper and a pen. It means that the next time you're writing a paper for class, you check out additional resources at the library. You don't just interview one person as part of your research; you interview five.

The gift of overpreparing is not just that you can then overdeliver, catching people's attention and showing that you mean business. It also eliminates the stress of whether you'll be able to follow through on what is asked of you. You don't need to worry. You know you have put in the time, and thought through every scenario. You are as ready as you'll ever be. And that leads to confidence, which leads to conviction, which leads to people realizing that you are someone they want to keep working with.

EVERY JOB, BIG AND SMALL

Going above and beyond in every task given to you is a powerful tactic to rise faster and go farther. I experienced this firsthand when I was in college, starting at the *Yale Herald*. When I was brought on as the school newspaper's financial analyst, I knew that my "job" was really to manage the books, since the paper was facing impending bankruptcy and struggling to stay in circulation. I could see clearly from examining the numbers that there wasn't enough revenue coming in. The easiest solution: find recurring advertisers, companies that catered to a young adult crowd. When I approached the publisher with this idea, she loved it. But there was no one to implement this strategy—except me.

Here's a key component of crushing it: You have to realize that it is up to you. That there is no job too small to take on and perform perfectly. Whether it is making coffee, designing signs for a fundraiser, or planning an event for the student council, the people who rise quickly are the ones who are willing to do the grunt work. I promise that one day you'll graduate from the grunt work! But until that day, your bosses, friends,

ME WITH MY GOOD FRIEND ERIK, WITH WHOM I LED *THE YALE HERALD*.

teachers, and coaches will value you even more because you are willing to take on every job and treat it with the respect it deserves.

So I went door-to-door selling advertisements, and dollar by dollar we pulled ourselves out of debt. That willingness to dive right in, identify the problem, and solve it myself led to me being named publisher of the *Herald* just months later.

And it didn't stop there. After my tenure at the *Herald*, because I'd not only pulled the paper out of impending bankruptcy but eventually filled the ranks with talented and driven students who could keep the paper profitable long after I left, I was approached to help manage some of the dramatic productions at Yale. Most of the people working in the drama department were creatives—geniuses, really—but they needed a business-minded individual to step in and help them manage the budget, the crew, ticketing, marketing, and more. It was yet another lesson for me in what it takes to run a business toward profit. And it was yet another

opportunity to practice my skills in crushing it.

Soon after that, I joined the founding team behind the *Misfit*. Again, people had seen my successes—with the *Herald* and dramatic productions—and were looking for a business-minded individual to help them develop their business model. When I came on board, I went above and beyond, not only helping to sell out the advertising space within the publication but also helping with the recruitment of other team members and the build-out of operations, marketing, and distribution. This enabled the organization to thrive even beyond its initial vision and, in turn, I developed lifelong friendships with the other girls on the team, which led to even more friendships and collaborations down the line, on campus and in life.

Each experience I had at Yale seemed to stem from the one before. It was my ability to see the big picture, take on problems big and small, and crush it in everything I was doing that led to more jobs, more responsibility,

EMBRACE THE
SIDE HUSTLE

Another component of crushing it is to always be on the lookout for opportunities to learn and expand your growth. Some people call these jobs "side hustles," or work that you do aside from your full-time job to either pull in more money or to actually pursue your passions.

It doesn't matter what age you are: Don't let it hold you back. You can be a teenager and have double or triple the number of jobs and side hustles that your peers in college or even graduate school have had. Jobs like helping out at an animal shelter, organizing fundraisers, designing a friend's website, volunteering at a food pantry, being general manager of the school musical. These are all valuable experiences that teach you important skills that you can apply to future employment.

I know that being willing to take on all these additional side hustles outside of my primary job or responsibility at the time helped to accelerate me personally and professionally. It allowed me to build friendships with top industry leaders and to be hired into higher-level internships and jobs than I might have ever otherwise received at the time. It gave investors confidence in my abilities when I went to pitch them Mogul, and ultimately allowed me to feel ready to launch my own company when others from the outside might have deemed me too young.

and more opportunities. Because when you know how to crush it, people always want you on their team!

GOING THE EXTRA MILE

It was while I was at Harvard Business School that I met Ann Sarnoff, the president of BBC Studios Americas. She was an HBS alum, and during my second year there, I was invited to become a consultant for her coproductions and acquisitions team. What that really meant was that my team was tasked with making the BBC show *Sherlock* a success in the US. Nowadays, the show has amassed a massive fandom among young people everywhere. But at the time, the show's fate in the US was not so obvious. And while some shows translate easily, for others you have to study the market and see what aspects of the show will resonate most with the audience you are seeking to reach. The questions for my team were, What audiences were the BBC not yet reaching, and how could we approach them with

this show to bring them into the fold?

During my time as a consultant for the BBC, I was always looking for more that I could do. I wanted to see things that others weren't seeing, identify opportunities, and drive them forward. I wanted to come up with new ways to poll potential viewers, new avenues for outreach, and innovative ways to solve other challenges the BBC would be facing with the show in the US.

Years later, the BBC invited me to be its speaker for International Women's Day, in the form of a fireside chat with Ann before a global audience. It was surreal to be welcomed back in this way, now as the CEO of Mogul. The fireside chat took place in the network's New York headquarters, but was simulcast to its various offices around the world, including Miami, Mexico City, LA, and Toronto. And I relayed this same advice: to always be looking for how you could go above and beyond in the job you've been given. Sometimes that means looking outside your department to see how else you could be of service, searching for opportunities to collaborate with

RETURNING TO BBC AS THEIR KEYNOTE SPEAKER FOR INTERNATIONAL WOMEN'S DAY.

other coworkers. I never wanted to be known as a specialist in just one thing, but to be someone who wasn't afraid to step in on any project, to cross the boundaries of departments and reach out to see how a new collaboration could unlock an entirely new opportunity.

After our fireside chat ended, Ann forwarded me a note from a young man in the BBC's Canadian office who had been deeply inspired by my words. He also had Vietnamese parents and sometimes worried about his tendency to be a generalist in his work. He was grateful that I had encouraged him to cast his net widely in terms of potential avenues for growth.

People take notice when you are willing to work your hardest. In a world where many people seem to expect things to be handed to them, you will set yourself apart if you are one of the few who always work hard, have no ego, volunteer for additional responsibility, are always overprepared, and always overdeliver on every task. This will get you noticed in classes, sports, career, and life.

Obviously, this attitude came with me to Mogul, and those days when I was barely sleeping were a testament to the fact that I was going to give my company—my baby—just as much attention and care and love as every other job I'd taken on to date. Mogul's growth was thanks to a commitment to stay connected to our early users, to stay focused on our mission, and to overdeliver to those clients who took a chance on us early on.

I tend to hire people who have this mind-set as well. We have a lot of high school and college super-users at Mogul who reach out to us, wanting to contribute to our mission in any way. Those who show us that they know how to crush it are sometimes invited to be summer interns, during which time we teach them the ins and outs of the team they have joined. But they always go above and beyond, without us even asking. If photos need to be edited, they teach themselves how to use editing software and then deliver amazing photos. If we are hosting an event for the Mogul community, they will jump into any volunteer role needed for those hours, all hands on deck. We've hired many interns full-time once they graduate, or otherwise recommended them for jobs at NASA, Facebook, and Salesforce, and top graduate programs at Harvard and Oxford.

We've also had high school students reach out to me or the team, and then become absolute rock stars. I received the letter below from a fifteen-year-old girl from Bucharest, Romania. And as you'll see, she took a page from my fangirl playbook:

Hello,
My name is Sofia, I'm a high school student from Bucharest, Romania, interested in collaborating with Mogul to empower women from Romania and make their voices heard.

I believe this partnership would bring so many new members to the Mogul platform, but most importantly will offer Romanian girls and women a safe place where they could share thoughts and receive advice. As a young girl growing up in Romania, a second world country known for its discrimination and lack of representation of minorities, I know how difficult it is for women and young girls to receive the advice and help they need, access opportunities that others in more developed countries can reach within seconds, share thoughts without fear of judgment, and feel the love and support of a community of strong and inspiring women that will always have your back.

What I am proposing is dedicating a little corner of Mogul to the women of Bucharest, my home city (or maybe start a little smaller at a high school level) where all of those things would become possible. I could "run" this community and bring dozens of young girls and women to your platform, encouraging them to post and discuss while empowering them and inspiring them to create and pursue their passions.

I am the right person to run this initiative for multiple reasons. Firstly, I am an advocate for women's rights and equality and have been fighting for years to create change in my home country, despite the negativity and backlash. I am an active member of my community, volunteering and working to create a better city, and have also brought together my high school community through my blog, which has just under 20,000 readers. I also know and have worked with many incredible Romanian women of all ages and from all walks of life. Secondly, I have a lot of experience with journalism and publishing, as I have written for multiple magazines, have recently had my first book published and am currently working as an intern at *Glamour* magazine, despite being just 15 and a high school student. Thirdly, and most importantly, I am a lover of Mogul and its mission, and would be absolutely honored to work alongside its amazing team.

I believe that together, if this partnership were to come true, we would be able to create some incredible change in my home country, so I look forward to hearing from you, and if there's anything else you'd like to know about me or my idea, I'd be thrilled to answer any of your questions via email or via phone.

Best,
Sofia

Of course, after this email, we invited Sofia to join Mogul, and she went above and beyond to support the platform in every way possible. This past year, she was honored by our community for her tremendous contributions toward our mission during our annual Mogul X conference. As part of the award, she received an opportunity to share her story with the global audience. I could tell right away that she was a Girl Mogul in the making and that, with the right support, she could truly change the world.

You, too, have the ability to be someone people can count on, and when you become their go-to for any kind of project, you develop a relationship of trust, respect, and collaboration. Who knows? One day your role model or mentor might offer you your dream job because you were loyal, dependable, and helpful every step of the way.

Change the world.

THE ABC'S
OF
OVERDELIVERING

Understand the task given to you, and then ask yourself what else might be helpful to the person you are working for.

Do the initial task, then do the extra things as well.

Cut the deadline given to you in half.

If they ask for edits by the end of the week, see if you can get them back in two days. Or even overnight. You don't want to work so quickly that your work isn't the best quality. But you do want to show them that you prioritize their work and their time. You want to exhibit your ability to do an amazing job even with a quick turnaround time.

Put on your entrepreneur's hat.

Think creatively about the task given to you. Is there a way to innovate or do something more efficiently?

DANIELLE PANABAKER

ACTRESS AND STAR OF *THE FLASH*

DANIELLE PANABAKER

© David Livingston/Getty Images

I've been doing what I love from a very young age, and I feel so fortunate that I was able to start down this path early on. This business is filled with rejection, and I've been turned down more times than I've been hired. But you've got to be stubborn enough to keep showing up. You've got to keep hustling, because nothing in life comes easily. Especially when you are chasing your dreams.

When a rejection would come my way or I faced an obstacle, I focused on the mantra *This too shall pass*. And it allowed me to feel sad in the moment but remember that this was just one moment. More triumphs were to come.

I work on my craft every single day. It still doesn't always come naturally. I sometimes break out in hives when I get nervous. But why would you do something that didn't challenge you? Would you just want to be bored? Do you just want to do what you know you can, or do you want to push yourself? Every time I get through a scene, I feel this sense of accomplishment. I think it is important to enjoy the moment after. To say: *I did*

it! I was scared, and it was okay!

Each role I take on is one more challenge to conquer, one more way to grow and learn and evolve. I show up on set every day, and I'm never late. I seriously set like eighteen alarm clocks because I don't want to be late and make people wait. Even though I'm a bit of a control freak, I have chosen a career that can often feel like I don't have any control at all. So I'm constantly working on myself and growing as a person. I'm trying to learn to enjoy these moments of uncertainty, because I know that I could never plan out the amazing adventure that awaits me. **I'm going to keep doing what I'm doing, keep doing what I love, knowing that I'll never give up and that I will always work to be prepared for the next opportunity that comes my way.** ♛

CHAPTER ELEVEN
TAKING IT TO THE BANK

Beyoncé says girls run the world, and I couldn't agree more. But there's something else that makes the world go around, something else you need to know how to handle to become a Girl Mogul: money.

Money is a necessary component of our world, and unless you plan to go off the grid, you're going to need to learn a lot about it: how to earn it, manage it, save it, and invest it. Money management is an important skill set that young people are not often equipped with. We go from our parents' paying our bills to college, where they may still be paying at least some of the bills, to the real world, where, all of a sudden, you find yourself responsible for all the things that keep you alive, which includes food, shelter, health care, and more. Once you start really paying all your bills yourself, you realize just how many bills there are to pay.

Many women struggle through their teens and twenties, learning money lessons the hard way. But I think if you are prepared early on, before you venture out into the world on your own, you can avoid the kinds of mistakes that can set you back for years. The sooner you start saving, the sooner you can stop! It's true. The more money you set aside now—when you are young—the longer it can grow. You will find yourself with resources to access when you are ready to take the next leap—in order to go to college, build your own business, or buy a home.

It's never too early to get smart about money. So stick with me here, and you'll be thanking me later.

WHAT ARE YOU SAVING FOR?

I wasn't born with a silver spoon in my mouth, and I always knew how hard my parents were working to provide for us. It was that example of hard work, discipline, and the willingness to do what it takes to provide for those you love that taught me how to work hard for every penny. And to never take those pennies for granted.

I learned the value of a dollar early on, because I knew firsthand how much my parents were sacrificing for the family. And at a young age, my siblings and I made a pact: One day, we were going to be able to show them how thankful we were for all they had given us.

This attitude of giving back to one's parents is part of my family's culture. In Asia, it is traditional to find several generations living together. The parents, once they reach a certain age, move in with their children, to help take care of their grandchildren while also recognizing that their own kids will eventually be taking care of them. It is the circle of life. It is expected, a part of the fabric of society, and my parents, though no longer living in Asia, followed that example.

My parents sent every extra penny they earned while living in France back to their families. It was important to my parents that they stay connected, and that they provide for their parents and siblings as much as possible, as much as they also tried to provide for us. When we moved to Plano, my siblings and I knew it was in part so that we might have the best education possible, and more opportunities than we could ever imagine. My parents did it willingly, happily, joyously. They personified kindness in every way to their family and to others around them.

I know that example seeped into our consciousness as we were raised under their roof and with their values. By the

Money brings you freedom, not happiness.

time my sister, Kym, was preparing to leave for college, we decided that we were each going to do everything we could to become successful. We motivated each other with a friendly sibling competition to see who would become the first self-made millionaire. And it wasn't so that we could drive fancy cars or live an extravagant lifestyle. We wanted to be become successful so that, together, we would be able to use our collective funds to give back to our parents. We'd seen them sacrifice their own wishes and needs so that they could provide us with sports equipment, classes, and lessons. We envisioned being able to have them live near wherever we ended up, so that they could live well and know that we were taking care of them. We didn't want them to have any reason to worry about the future. We wanted them to know that their children would create the safety net they had always provided for us.

I learned early on that money should not be something you just accumulate. For me, it has always been a tool that you can use to create good in the world, and to take care of those whom you love.

My dad always emphasizes that money brings you freedom, not happiness. Money allows you to have the freedom of choice. If anything ever goes wrong in your career, you can leave without being constrained by lack of funds. You can chart your path forward because you're not dependent on that paycheck. If you have resources, you can do anything in the world that you truly wish—live your best life, become the best version of yourself, and truly create an impact on the world.

When I left CBS to focus on coding, the only reason I could do so was that I had amassed a rainy-day fund; I knew I could afford a few months of runway before I would really be in trouble if I couldn't find a way to monetize Mogul. I'm so thankful that I learned early on to find a cause that I was saving toward and the importance of having money saved up so that if I ever needed to, I could make a leap of faith. These lessons allowed me to start living the life I had always dreamed of.

HOW TO
EARN
MONEY

I know it can be hard to find opportunities to earn money when you are young. You are still going to school full-time, you may not have learned to drive (or have a car to take you anywhere), and many of the opportunities for youth pay only minimum wage. But every dollar counts. My sister, Kym, was superindustrious when she was in high school. She worked as a waitress, hostess, and grocery store clerk throughout high school. Me? I never really felt comfortable driving (I still don't drive to this day—but, of course, I live in New York City, where that is not unusual!), so I had to find different ways to earn money. I thought about what I enjoyed doing and what I was good at. One of my jobs was as a French tutor. I was a native French speaker, so the subject was easy for me. Plus I love to teach and mentor. I tutored a girl who would come to my house, and her parents paid me forty dollars an hour! I was doing what I loved, earning money, and didn't have to drive anywhere.

I also always competed in the school science fair. I often won first place, which came with a cash prize. Companies would sponsor additional prizes, which I would win as well. Once I won the school science fair, I could compete in the district science fair, then the regional science fair, then the state science fair. And each prize came with money attached. I saved hundreds of dollars this way, while also adding valuable bullet points to my college applications.

These days, with the internet and social enterprise, there is no limit to how you can monetize your efforts. Here are a few ideas to get you started:

Sell products online. Are you crafty and creative? Could you create an Etsy business? What about designing T-shirts on Zazzle?

Could you work to resell unwanted items, either from your own home, or your neighborhood? Tell your neighbors you are raising money for your college fund, and ask if they have anything they'd like to donate that you could sell online for cash.

Look into online errand services like TaskRabbit, so that you can make money doing odd jobs in your neighborhood. Sometimes elderly neighbors just need someone to help with weeding or moving furniture, simple things that you could easily assist with.

Don't neglect the tried-and-true money earners of the past! Babysitting, retail, restaurants, lawn-mowing, and dog-walking.

BE MINDFUL WITH YOUR MONEY

When I applied to college, I didn't tell my parents where I submitted my applications. I used money that I had earned through science fair competitions and various odd jobs to pay for the application fees, and I didn't visit any of the campuses before being accepted. I knew that I would need to receive scholarship money in order to go to some of my "reach" schools. If I didn't receive enough scholarship money to afford to go, I didn't want my parents to know. Because I knew they would try to sacrifice something so that I could have every opportunity life afforded me.

When I received my acceptance letters, I was thrilled. But I knew the next step was calling the financial aid offices. Each of the schools had awarded me some scholarship money, but I knew that I needed more. And so I called them up and thanked them for their generosity but stated clearly that it would be challenging for me to enroll unless they supplemented my financial aid

Nothing more ever comes unless you ask for it.

package. I made sure to be gracious and appreciative of what they had already given. But I was firm with what I needed. "Oh, of course, let me see what we can do," was often the response. And at every school, they came back to me with additional resources.

This is one of the most important skills you can learn when it comes to money. When you are hired for a part-time job and you are offered a certain wage, ask for more. When you are accepted to a camp but you know the fees will stretch your family's budget, ask if the camp offers scholarships.

The worst they can say is no. It can be hard for some people to advocate for themselves, so practice asking. Ask about discounts at stores. Ask for more information about a class project, or ask a classmate to help. Ask for extra-credit assignments. Ask for more. And then be gracious whether the answer is yes or no.

If you get good at this skill early on, it will automatically translate once you enter the workforce and are negotiating for bigger things, like salaries, promotions, and more.

It comes down to this: You should never leave money on the table.

You may receive some flak for asking for more. Sometimes people don't like it when you know your worth! But as long as you request in a respectful manner, you aren't doing anything wrong. Remember that. And maybe when the next person asks them for more, they will remember saying no to

you and they'll begin to realize that they aren't offering enough.

When I received my acceptance to Harvard Business School, I did the same thing. I called the financial aid office and asked what it could do. I ended up receiving a full scholarship for the entire first year, and I paid for my second year with loans.

Because you've worked hard to earn your money or to get that scholarship, you also want to be mindful with the money that you do spend. You want to be sure that every dollar that leaves your piggy bank is going toward an expense that is worthwhile. Ideally, you want to spend your money on experiences and opportunities that will benefit you for years to come. So, yes, spend your money on a camp that will teach you important skills and connect you with influential people. Spend your money on travel, which will expand your horizons and worldview, and teach you more than any book could. Spend your money on applications to college, on education, classes, and internships.

And then save the rest, so that you

ESTABLISHING
A RAINY-DAY
FUND

One of the most important things you can do right now is ensure that you have a checking account and a savings account. I got my first account when I was fourteen. But even if you are younger than that, ask your parents to help you sign up for one at their bank so that you have somewhere to deposit your money. At a certain point, you're going to outgrow that piggy bank on your shelf. Plus, it is such a thrilling thing to see your money accumulating in the account over time, and with online banking, it's easier than ever. When I was younger, I tried to save 80 percent of what I was earning. I would leave 20 percent in my checking account for random spending needs, and everything else I would save and watch as I kept adding to it. Here's how to get started:

Track your spending. Take one month and keep track of everything you spent. Yes, *everything.* From a Starbucks run to a download on Apple Music to those new jeans. You can write it in a notebook or in one of the free budgeting apps available on your phone (Mint, Fudget, Goodbudget, and Pennies to name just a few).

Take note of where your money went during that month. You may be surprised at how some things add up. Now multiply that number by 12, and that's an estimate of how much you spend in one year. It is important to see your spending habits. Only by acknowledging the choices that you are currently making can you determine if changes need to be made.

See if you can cut back on some of your spending habits so that you can establish your rainy-day fund. Your rainy-day fund may be money that you tap into for a trip you've been dreaming about. It could be saving up to assist a special family member that you know needs some help. It could be saving for college. Identify your goal, and then aim to set aside at least 10 percent of the money you make for that rainy-day fund. See if you can be like me and save even more! If the money is in your checking account, you are likely to just spend it. Transferring it from checking to savings protects it and allows it to grow over time as you add more and more from every paycheck, allowance, birthday gift, or prize you receive.

can have the rainy-day fund you need to have the freedom to go after your dreams.

A WORD ON DEBT

Yes, I said before that I took out student loans so that I could pay for that final year of business school. And it was hard, for a couple of years postgraduation, to have those payments due. But I knew that having that degree was important to my future earning power—and for me to gather the confidence and skills to launch my own company one day. Those loans were an investment.

Still, you have to be careful about how much debt you take on. More and more these days, people are questioning whether a college degree is even necessary, considering how much debt students are burdened with upon graduation. And I agree that something needs to be done. The experiences, classes, and colleagues that I gained from college were priceless, and opened up opportunities that would have been

hard to come by someplace else. You may be pursuing different kinds of dreams, so it may be technical training, living in another country for valuable research experience, or an arts program that you need—but it all requires funding in some way, and you may need to borrow money.

Learning how to manage debt is an important skill. Our financial world is based on the loaning and paying back of money. In fact, the only way to establish good credit is by having a credit card and paying the balance off in full each month. What is "good credit"? It is a system our financial world uses to assess whether you are safe to loan money to. You need good credit to get a loan to buy a house or a car. You need good credit to rent an apartment. If you have "bad credit" (i.e., you were not dependable in paying back money you borrowed over time), it can stick with you for years.

One easy way to start figuring out how to manage debt is to sign up for a credit card. Now, this is something you'll have to do with the cooperation and sign-off of your parents. If they don't think you are ready now, talk to them about how old they think you should be before they will allow this responsibility. Tell them that you are just trying to learn how to budget, save, and pay off balances. And this is key! You always want to pay off your credit-card balance every month.

Don't get into the habit of buying things you cannot afford. Why? When you keep a balance on your credit card, the company charges you interest on that money, which you essentially are still borrowing. Paying interest on your credit-card balance is like giving the credit-card company all your hard-earned money.

Say, for example, you found a really incredible pair of jeans that you just had to have. You don't have $100 at the time to pay for them with cash, so you put it on your credit card. Great! That means you have about thirty days to gather the funds.

But say at the end of thirty days, when your credit-card statement comes and the balance is due, you don't have that money. The credit-card company will allow you to pay off just some of what you owe (called the "minimum balance"). Say the minimum balance is $25. Great! Then you have another thirty days to acquire the next $75.

But you have to pay interest on that $75. Credit-card interest rates vary, from 15 percent to over 20 percent. So when that next credit-card statement

Have a rainy-day fund.

IS IT WORTH IT?

You will face a number of important decisions in your early life regarding whether to take on large debt. This can include decisions about whether to go to college, where to go to college, what kind of car to buy, and what size of apartment to rent. When deciding between different opportunities, try to ask yourself the question *Is it worth it?* Is the new car with a car payment of $500 a month worth it? Or could you save up and pay cash for a used car, and no longer have the recurring payment? Same with an apartment: While you love the thought of having your own space, is the extra $400 a month worth it as opposed to finding some roommates to share with? Sometimes the answer is yes! But by asking the question, you do a check-in and make sure you are being thoughtful about what kind of monetary commitment you are agreeing to.

You may not be facing these kinds of big-money questions yet, but train yourself to ask these questions about the smaller things as well so that you learn the skills of being mindful with your money.

comes, you owe not just $75. If you have a 15 percent interest rate, now an additional $11.25 in interest is owed, or a total of $86.25. If your interest rate is 20 percent, you owe an additional $15, or a total of $90.

So you've bought yourself a bit of time, but now those jeans cost you not $100, but $111.25 or $115. Interest can add up. Fast. So avoid accumulating a balance on your credit card. You don't want to be paying interest. Ever.

Making the right decisions about debt early on is essential to your future success. You may not care about debt right now, but learning about it—practicing taking on debt and paying it back—will provide you with the skills to do so later, when you are dealing with bigger amounts and larger repercussions.

MONETIZING MOGUL

The only reason that I was able to quit my job at CBS to commit to Mogul full-time was because I had amassed a small rainy-day fund that I knew could sustain me until Mogul started to bring in money of its own. Without that cushion, I wouldn't have been able to take that essential leap.

But I also knew that it wouldn't last long. So from the very start, I focused on how to monetize Mogul in a way that didn't detract from its mission. I knew that, as a startup, we would be approaching investors, but I never wanted to be dependent on their money. I wanted Mogul to be self-sustaining.

The first step I took was to sell advertisements on our site. I went first to one of the loyal advertisers and friends that I had cultivated while at the *Herald*—Soraya, the owner of York Street Noodle House in New Haven. Because she had helped me by buying advertisements in the *Herald*, I had committed to helping her business by bringing in students to the restaurant, so much so that it became a staple for me and I was there multiple times a week for years. We'd become good friends and supporters of each other's causes. She agreed to advertise with Mogul right away. So the first $500 arrived in the bank account.

Once David, Namisha, Bethany, Juli, and Natasha joined the team, we formed a department focused on creating marketing campaigns for clients: Mogul Studios. We combined our expertise and contacts to reach out to female company founders who we hoped might take a chance on our new company. We had to approach a lot of them before we got a yes. But one client led to another client, which led to another client.

Though for our first client we were

paid only $2,000 for twenty pieces of content, by our third client we were charging $35,000, and we continued to grow. Today, we are lucky enough to have many Fortune 1000 companies as clients, and we are often bidding for jobs alongside giants like Facebook and LinkedIn. I love being the underdog, and I love when we win the campaign.

But as we continue to grow, I have never forgotten one of the most important lessons I learned from business school: You want to have several streams of revenue in case one ever dries up. After the launch of Mogul Studios, and once we had several investors on board, we created Mogul Learning. It offers e-learning courses to provide women with concrete guidance on how to rise in their careers, what it takes to be an entrepreneur, the ins and outs of higher education, money management, and more. These are courses that we have tailored specifically for Mogul's users, and it's the very information that girls came to me for in those early days when I was receiving hundreds of emails. We charge a small fee

for each course as an additional way for Mogul to earn revenue, and we provide ongoing support for each person who signs up for a course.

As Mogul's user base began to grow and Mogul Studios began to work with Fortune 1000 companies on marketing campaigns, these very companies wanted to be able to reach our user base, because it held the exact pool of talent that they wanted for their companies. They began to ask whether they could create profiles on Mogul, to post jobs and talk about their corporate culture, so that they might attract the future employees they knew were already active on our site and looking for new opportunities. Mogul At Work was born, a program in which companies pay a subscription fee for the right to post content and jobs on our platform. Today, we collaborate with thousands of human-resources leaders and departments across the globe.

Each of these different divisions began to bring in revenue, while at the same time enhancing and expanding the overall mission of Mogul. I was

Money on its own is meaningless.

money that makes it truly valuable.

Obviously, I believe that more and more women should be empowered to start their own companies, become CEOs, and be promoted to positions of power and prestige. And one of the quickest ways you can become equipped for the business world is to understand money—how to earn it, how to ask for it, and how to grow it. Money can mean freedom for many, and it can definitely help you become a Girl Mogul.

INVEST IN YOUR FUTURE

You may be aware of the wage gap between men and women. Equal pay for equal work is something women are still fighting for to this day. The statistics are discouraging: According to the National Partnership for Women & Families, for every dollar Caucasian men earn for doing the same job, Caucasian women earn 79 cents, African American women just 60 cents, and Hispanic women just

never going to sacrifice mission for money. Yes, money was important and would allow us to grow even more. But first and foremost was the vision that I'd had when I started this company. With each new initiative, I asked myself if it would empower women; if it would provide them with much needed resources, support, and opportunities; or if it would expand horizons for women and help them reach positions of power and prominence. If the answer was yes, then I would move forward.

You never want to pursue money for money's sake. Money on its own is meaningless. It is what you do with

55 cents. Asian American women are doing the best of all their counterparts: 87 cents for every dollar Caucasian men earn. But all of these disparities truly add up. Mogul, along with many other companies, is doing everything we can to address this issue in varied ways. This is one of the reasons I want you to remember to ask for more. Men notoriously have less of an issue demanding higher pay, thus they make more from the start.

I'm not sure why it is that women are nervous about asking for more or being seen as desiring wealth. For men, it has always been a sign of prestige, but women have been taught not to seek wealth. Again, I don't think money should ever be pursued just to accumulate wealth, but when we are afraid of asking for money or seeking money, we can find ourselves at the back of the pack.

And while you may not have a lot of control over the wage gap, you do have more control over something called the "investment gap." Men are more likely than women to invest their money, which means their money has the potential to grow faster. Now, investing your money doesn't mean you need to become a whiz at the stock market and check the Dow Jones Industrial Average every morning. To invest your money means that you do more than just sock your money away in a savings account in a bank, which typically earns very little interest (less than 1 percent). When you invest your money, you give it the potential to grow at a much higher rate, sometimes as much as 7–8 percent per year. This is something that you will likely have to talk to your parents about and have them help you with. Maybe they know a lot about investing and can even provide some tips. Or maybe your interest in the topic will nudge them to get educated as well. It can be something you do together.

Remember the interest that I said you wanted to avoid with credit cards by paying off your balance each month? Well, you can make interest work *for* you if you invest your money. This is when compound interest is your friend! When you save money in an account

Starting early can have huge advantages.

that earns interest and don't make any withdrawals, you're earning interest not only on your initial investment but also on the interest itself.

Let me give you a concrete example so that you can see how quickly earning interest can work for you. Say you have a great-aunt who passes away and leaves you $10,000. (I'm so sorry for your loss, but let's take advantage of the gift she has given you.) If you invest that $10,000 in an account that earns 10 percent interest (that's a bit higher than your average account earns, but it makes the math much easier!), by the end of the year, you'll have $11,000 in that account. Great! You just made $1,000 doing nothing.

During the second year you hold this account, you'll be earning 10 percent interest on $11,000 instead of only $10,000, so you'll now have $12,100 at the end of the year. At the end of the third year, you'll have $13,310. All without saving another dollar. You are just tapping into the power of compound interest.

If you save that $10,000 for ten years at 10 percent, you'll end up with $25,937.

Now, 10 percent is the kind of growth that you will see in the stock market. Not every investment has that high of a return. But you can see how starting early can have huge advantages. The earlier you invest, the more that compound interest works for you. In fact, even if you stop investing at an early age, and let the money you've already set aside utilize the power of compound interest, you could end up with a bigger nest egg than someone who starts later and saves for many more years.

Again, don't feel like you have to understand all the ins and outs of the stock market in order to invest. You can identify a trusted adult who can help guide you through the process once you determine that you have a rainy-day fund large enough that you are not going to need to access it for a couple of years. Tell them you'd like to make the most of that money that you saved and ask whether they could help you determine how to best invest it.

Here are some options. You can invest your savings in a "low-cost index fund," which is a conglomeration of many stocks. In fact, the most famous investor in the world, Warren Buffett, recommends this kind of investment. For a very small fee, your money can grow at a rate of roughly 7 percent per year (when the stock market is performing well on average). Or you can put your money in a CD (a certificate of deposit), a savings account where your money can earn interest at a guaranteed rate

of 2 percent per year, but you'll have to agree to leave it there for a certain amount of time.

Getting past your fear of investing while you are still under the guidance of adults will serve you well in the long term. We don't know exactly why women are less likely than men to invest their money, though some think that women may be more hesitant because they don't want to risk losing everything. The truth is, a study by Fidelity referenced in *Money* magazine noted that women are better investors than men, overall making a return 1 percent higher than men; they don't panic during down cycles, they don't overtrade, and they work hard to pay less in fees than their male counterparts.

The investing gap can add up even faster than the wage gap—costing you up to a million dollars in your lifetime. This is in part due to the fact that women keep a full 71 percent of their assets in cash, according to a 2016 survey by the investment firm BlackRock, while men keep just 60 percent in cash. While investing can be risky, keeping

FURTHER READING

Mogul Learning has developed an entire course on personal finance. Filled with fun GIFs and easy-to-digest information, it will allow you to dig even deeper on how to make your money work for you.

all your assets in cash means that you are limiting its ability to grow. After all, $10,000 in the bank remains just that—$10,000 in the bank.

Obviously, how to invest wisely is a book in itself. But I highly recommend finding someone in your life that you can talk to about investing, and also that you continue to do research. The earlier you start, the more you'll make.

SUZE ORMAN

INTERNATIONALLY ACCLAIMED PERSONAL FINANCE ICON, HOST OF *THE SUZE ORMAN SHOW,* AND AUTHOR OF *WOMEN & MONEY*

I was no more than eight years old, sitting in my father's store, where he and my grandfather sold chickens. Every day I sat with them until the last chicken had been sold, and we could—finally—go home.

That day, I was so excited when I knew we were down to the last chicken that my father kept in the back of the store.

A woman walked in and asked if we had any chickens left.

My father said, "Yes," as he walked into the back room where the chickens were kept.

He emerged with the one chicken that was left and put it on the scale. He told the lady, "It will be a dollar."

She wasn't satisfied with that chicken, and asked my father, "Do you have any bigger ones?"

TIFFANY PHAM AND SUZE ORMAN

My father didn't miss a beat and said, "Well, let me go back and see."

I sat there on my stool, thinking, *Wait, there's only one chicken! What is my father talking about?*

THREE GENERATIONS OF WORKING WOMEN: LITTLE SUZE, MOM, AND GRANDMA GOLDIE!

He picked up the one chicken from the scale and returned to the back room. He then returned—with the exact same chicken—put it on the scale, looked at the woman and said, "This one will be a dollar seventy-five."

I couldn't believe what my father was doing, and then the lady said: "Great, I'll take both of them."

I thought *Oh my god*. He had been caught in his lie. I was so afraid I ran out of the store.

In that moment of fear, I learned a lesson that has guided me my entire life. I was just a little girl, but I knew right then and there that you must always stand in your truth, and tell the truth. Lies just lead to trouble. **It was in that moment of my father's chicken lie that I made the decision to always do what is right, not just what seems easy. It is the key to why I am a Mogul today.** ♟

CHAPTER TWELVE
SPEAKING UP

I used to think of a leader as someone who was bigger and louder than everyone else. Because that was my frame of reference for what a leader looked like, it was hard to envision myself as one. I was shy and soft-spoken and, in high school, oftentimes unsure of my ideas.

Today, I'm a gregarious introvert. I'm definitely still soft-spoken, but I am no longer unsure of my ideas. I know I have something to say, and I'm not afraid to share it. I no longer think I have to be the loudest in the room in order to be a leader. I know that a leader can be just as powerful listening quietly, then speaking with conviction. A leader is someone who isn't afraid to use their voice and identify new ways of doing things.

It is imperative as women that we learn to use our voices, add them to the conversation, and see ourselves as leaders from the very start. This is the only way that we will change the power dynamics that are still in play in our society one hundred years after women were granted the right to vote, and fifty-five years after we were promised equal pay.

Anyone can be a leader and use their voice to change the world.

CULTIVATE CONVICTION

One of the best ways to gain confidence in using your voice is to practice using it every chance you are given. This could be in a poetry reading, in the classroom, in student council, or at science fairs. My freshman year of high school, when I began to research the detrimental effect of pesticides on the environment for my science fair project, I learned not just the value of researching a topic but also what it was like to present my findings persuasively to a group of people. Obviously, the need for pesticides was never going to go away, but I began to wonder if we might be able to find a less destructive way to repel insects. Could we find natural repellents, occurring in nature, that would do the same job without the devastating impact?

My sophomore year, I expanded on this concept and had data that backed up what I was saying. I also began to develop a story around it—a story that brought home the personal impact of what the chemicals were doing not just to our world but to our town, our waters, and our children. I spoke of the impact Rachel Carson's highly lauded book *Silent Spring* had had on me, and how I had been determined to fight for the environment's well-being ever since.

I poured myself into the research and figuring out the best way to present my findings at the fair. But my least favorite part was the presentation itself. I dreaded standing in front of the judges and trying to convey what I had discovered.

Still, by my junior year, I had so much data, and so much passion for the story of how this could truly change the world, that I spoke out clearly and concisely, and appealed personally to the judges about the global impact of developing natural pesticides. And I won first place—not only at the school fair but then again at the city, regional, and state fairs.

Each time I gave my presentation, I gained confidence from having been rewarded with recognition the time before. But I also began to realize that though my voice was quieter than some, it carried conviction. Instead of focusing on the volume of my voice, I focused on conveying how deeply I cared.

I didn't have to be the loudest one in the room, after all. I just had to show the people I was talking to that my words mattered (and get them out of my mouth without choking).

The more that you feel truly convinced that the opinions brewing in your mind matter, the more you'll realize how you can no longer hold them back. To use your voice means to call out what is wrong in the world. To share your opinion means to engage in the world and provide a solution or idea that is desperately needed. To join the conversation means you don't just sit back and let others solve problems. You step up, into the fray, into the discussion, and become a change-maker.

To be a leader, you can't swallow your opinions. You must voice them.

PRACTICE MAKES PERFECT

You don't have to speak at your high school graduation to practice using your voice. Start small and then get bigger. Raise your hand in class. When you are at an after-school activity and your coach asks a question, be the one who speaks up. If you want to take it further, you can join a debate team or audition for a school play. The more activities you volunteer for, the more you'll be presented with opportunities to add to the conversation. Pretty soon, you'll be so used to using your voice, it won't feel like something you have to practice; it will just come naturally.

CONTRIBUTING TO THE CONVERSATION

It wasn't until a few years into college that I really had to address my fears of speaking up in public on a daily basis. I double majored in economics and international studies, and most of my econ classes consisted of lectures, where class participation was at a minimum. But by my junior and senior years, when I took most of my international relations courses, the classes were small seminars, where participation was a huge part of your grade. Since there were just ten to fifteen students in the room, professors encouraged us to enter the discussion often. Other times, students would be subject to the "cold call"—when the professor calls on an unwitting, unsuspecting student and makes them answer a question, whether they know the answer or not.

I hated this practice. In my first few months of seminars, I tried to hide in my chair, dreading the cold call, my palms slick with sweat and my heart beating a mile a minute.

But I'm also so thankful for those years and those fears. Because I had to face them. I had to figure out a way to be prepared and confident if a professor called on me. I was never going to be like some of my classmates, who seemed happy to speak whether they had something to contribute to the discussion or not. So every night, I would write out on note cards the three main takeaways I had gleaned from the reading. I put them in bulleted form and wrote out what I would say word for word. So that if the professor happened to call on me the next day, I would not be shaking in my seat, but would be able to pull out my cue cards and speak up clearly, confidently, and with conviction.

Soon, I got to the point where I had prepared so well that I *wanted* the professor to call on me! And by the end of my senior year, I was honored with distinction by the international studies department.

In an interview with *The New York Times*, novelist Mary Gordon talked about how women are often so tentative and afraid to speak up: "I teach at a women's college, Barnard, across the street from Columbia, which used to be male for donkey's years, and I say to my students, 'Do not speak into your collar when you tell me your name. There are men across the street saying things of immense stupidity at the top of their lungs.'"

I don't know where we learn to be afraid of the sound of our voices. Perhaps it comes from a culture that still values timidity and meekness in girls and celebrates brashness and audacity in boys. But I created Mogul so that girls could know that their voices are valid, important, and essential to our world. That we don't need to sit back and wait to be called on. That we need to raise our hands and contribute to the conversation.

CREATING BUY-IN

There will always be times in your life when you need to use your voice. Whether you are speaking in front of a crowd or giving your opinion in a board meeting, you cannot avoid the need to use your voice and share it with the world.

And would you believe that I've now done it so much that I no longer think twice about speaking in public? In 2017, I had more than two hundred speaking engagements! And I relished every single one, because I loved the opportunity to meet so many Mogul users.

I got a lot of practice speaking persuasively in front of groups of people when I was pitching investors. Now, my first few pitches happened over the phone, with me sitting on my bed in my pajamas. But I eventually began to approach investors in person. I

SPEAKING WITH REPORTERS AT TECHCRUNCH DISRUPT.

CONVEYING PRESENCE AND CONFIDENCE

No matter whether you are giving a graduation speech in front of thousands or just giving a presentation in front of your class, there are tricks and techniques to convey presence and poise no matter how frightened you may be on the inside.

Look for friendly faces. Find someone in the room who you know loves and supports you and look at their face when you walk up onstage. Odds are that they will encourage you with a smile, which can give you the boost of confidence to stand tall, look at your note cards, and open your mouth.

Look people in the eye. Don't just stare at those note cards! Make sure that you are looking around your audience and trying to make eye contact. This conveys confidence and allows you to connect with the people listening directly. They may have been ignoring you, but as soon as their eyes meet yours, you know they'll start to tune in!

Slow down your words. Whenever I'm nervous, I start speaking quickly, like I'm trying to get through whatever I want to say so that I can rush offstage. Focus on your breathing and consciously slow yourself down, trying to enunciate each word so that it hits home, not only so people can hear and understand you but also to send a message of passion to your audience, and a message to your nerves that you aren't going to listen to them. You're the one in charge, and you are going to get through this confidently and with poise!

Incorporate gestures. No one enjoys watching a robot read from a piece of paper. Try to incorporate movements into your presentation, whether it is holding up numbers as you go through a list, or smacking your hand on the podium to make a point. It adds another dynamic element to your performance that is destined to make it stand out.

was invited to their companies and boardrooms, and soon found myself in situations that I had to admit were intimidating. Not just because this was my company and I wanted to secure the best investors possible but also because most investors are men, and they notoriously don't invest in women. When I pitched Mogul, only 10 percent of startup founders were female. And of the billions of dollars that venture capital firms invest in companies, from 2011 to 2013 only 3 percent of that money went to companies with a female CEO, according to a study published in the journal *Venture Capital*.

So, yes, I felt a bit intimidated. But I also knew the potential of this company. We'd been in existence for only a few short months, and we were already reaching one million women across 130 countries.

So I went back to the tool that had served me so well with that science fair project. I focused on the story of Mogul and used data to back it up. I kept it personal—talking about why I had built it, the influence of my family, and how desperately women needed a place to go to be supported and encouraged, to find mentors, and to discover resources, as our monumental growth attested. I walked into each pitch focused on three things: Why is this important to me? Why is this important to you? And why is this important to the world?

Remember when I first came up with that pattern? In those early days asking for clothing donations for Afghan children in high school! That pitch *still* works for me. And it can work for you. Be impassioned. Let them see how something affects you. Then turn your attention to them. How does this issue affect them in their lives personally? And finally, take it broad. How does this problem impede our world and truly have global impact?

This is how you create buy-in, whether from your peers, your parents, your coaches, your teachers, or your potential employers.

I also, of course, always over-prepare. Before each of those initial meetings, I thought about all the questions people might ask and objections they might raise. And I practiced my response to every single one. So that when I walked into each meeting, I felt confident and full of conviction; I knew that Mogul was going places, whether they would commit to investing or not.

Today, I'm invited to speak at events globally throughout the year, and it is something I truly enjoy. It was never something I was naturally gifted at, but I love the chance to encourage women. I stay focused on that—my why—and it keeps me going and gets me excited to step onto any stage.

So if you are afraid to speak up, just remember why you are doing it! Keep that purpose in front of you. Close your eyes and visualize your reason if you need to. Then raise your hand or step into the arena. And know that you have the power to change minds, change hearts, and change the world.

VALUE YOUR VOICE

I created Mogul as a user-generated platform because I wanted you to know that you have something to say, something to share, and that only *you* can say it! You can be a Girl Mogul by being 100 percent authentically you. Share your thoughts. Within you are ideas and projects and solutions that no one else will come up with in exactly the same way. Don't keep them to yourself. Share them with the world. Each time you do, you'll see how many people were helped, and you'll gain confidence to do it again and again. In order for more women to step into leadership positions, we have to learn to value our voices, use them frequently, and recognize how important they are to the conversation. Remember that we are done chasing perfectionism. We were born to take risks!

Becoming a Girl Mogul is not necessarily about becoming the first female president or running your own company. It's about understanding that you are an important, valuable person in the world who can exact amazing changes and impact the world in ways both big and small. It's about an invitation to know how much you have to offer and to no longer be afraid of what others will say. It is about joining the millions of women who have gone before you, are walking alongside you, and will follow in your footsteps to be the strongest, most courageous, most loving versions of themselves.

It is time for us all to rise up together and claim that power that has been in us all along.

We were born to take risks!

STRUCTURING
YOUR PITCH

Whether you want to create a side business and need to borrow some money from your family, or you are approaching the school board for additional resources for a certain department, or you are trying to hit it out of the park at a college interview, here are some tips to keep in mind:

Keep it personal. You want to connect with the people you are trying to convince, so make it clear how this is meaningful to you.

Back it up with data. Do your research. A personal plea is great, but you want to show that you've done the legwork to understand the details of the problem you are trying to address or solve. If you're at a college interview, make sure you understand the school's minimum requirements and how you more than fulfill them. Know what kinds of students the college is interested in and how you check each box.

Boil your argument down to three main points and keep repeating them. This may sound formulaic, but repetition really is important in order to emphasize your point and help your audience remember it well after you are gone.

Connect your goal to a greater one that everyone can get behind. Show how this is bigger than you.

ONE OF MY FIRST PRESS APPEARANCES, TALKING ABOUT MOGUL AT NASDAQ.

FLASHING A RARE GRIN WHILE ON MSNBC *YOUR BUSINESS* WITH MY FRIEND, TV HOST J.J. RAMBERG.

mogul mentor
VELLA LOVELL
ACTRESS AND STAR OF *CRAZY EX-GIRLFRIEND* AND *THE BIG SICK*

Ryan West

VELLA
LOVELL

Although I didn't realize it when I decided to pursue acting as a career, when you aim to be an actor, you inadvertently put yourself out there to be judged, ridiculed, targeted, loved, or hated. You cannot hide as an actor. Everything is exposed. And that can be scary. Especially when you are someone who doesn't look like everyone else.

When I studied theater at Juilliard, my appearance didn't really matter. We were doing Shakespeare and Chekhov, and, sure, those roles weren't necessarily created for someone who looks like me, but it was school, so you were cast, and no one made a big deal about it.

Once I started auditioning, however, I discovered that *everything* is about how you look. It doesn't matter how talented you are; casting directors often have a specific idea of what they want certain characters to look like. So the fact that I am a woman of color and that I'm ethnically ambiguous was something I had to deal with right from the start. In fact, many people assumed I was Indian or Southeast Asian. I'm mixed race—black, white, and a lot of other ethnicities probably mixed in. It was hard for a while when I realized that people were assuming I'm something that I'm not, and wanting to cast me in roles that weren't authentically me.

But the role of an actor is to step into other people's skin. I had to get comfortable with accepting that perhaps my ethnic ambiguity was a strength. In fact, it allowed me to be cast in the amazing indie hit *The Big Sick*, my first movie role, and a groundbreaking film in many, many ways.

Still, I loved that when I auditioned for the role of Heather in *Crazy Ex-Girlfriend*, her race was not specified.

The creators of the show didn't care whether she was a woman of color or not. And it felt amazing to just be able to portray a mixed-race girl on television. They even decided to focus one show on Heather's parents, how her father was African American and her mother was Caucasian. It allowed me to showcase my background, and made me realize that my ethnicity makes me unusual, and that can be a strength, not a weakness, something to celebrate rather than hide. There are a lot of girls in the world just like me. Girls who don't fit in a box. Girls who get mislabeled and misunderstood. I loved the chance to be able to show them a reflection of themselves on the screen. I hope that it makes them feel validated in a way that I never was when I was growing up.

Crazy Ex-Girlfriend allows me to show up as myself and make no apologies for who I am. (I promise, I am so much nicer than Heather, though there is a part of me that wishes that I could have some of her "I don't care" attitude!) There is a place for everyone in this world. Black, white, mixed, Asian, Latina, skinny, heavy, short, tall, there is no one "right" way to be in this world,

despite how much Hollywood tries to tell us otherwise.

I'm so lucky to be a part of a show that celebrates the amazing beauty of diversity and is breaking down boundaries. A show that isn't afraid to cast an Asian American man as a romantic lead, a show that isn't afraid to cast women who look like everyday women in leading roles, a show that isn't afraid to talk about mental health issues and the stuff that all women experience but are not *supposed* to talk about. It inspires me to be strong and funny and fearless in my endeavors. By putting myself out there, I hope that others can connect with me and my beautiful differentness, and that it allows them the space to be themselves.

We only get one life to live. Why would you spend it trying to be someone that you're not? The world needs girls who aren't afraid to be 100 percent who they are! We don't need carbon copies of what the world tells us we should be like. **The more that we are unafraid to be ourselves, the more amazing stories will be shared and the more we can all feel confident that who we are is enough.**

ACTION
STEPS

Congratulations on making it all the way through *Girl Mogul*! I hope you've received not just inspiration but some tangible tips to take with you as you navigate through your life. Information is power, but action is everything. You can read as many books as you want, but if they don't empower you to make some changes and do something new, you'll always stay in the same place!

So right now, flip through the book and do three exercises.

One, two, three—go!

Okay, now, are you done? Great! Those exercises gave you some ideas for changes to make, didn't they? Honestly, small actions can really add up.

The reason I wrote this book was so that you could see how much power you hold within you. The world needs girls like you—girls who know their worth, are tapped into their power, and aren't afraid to engage with the world. So, remember:

- You have so much awesomeness inside you waiting to emerge!
- Don't let anyone tell you that what matters is how you look! We both know now that it is about how you feel. So find the hacks that make you feel amazing, and watch the world take notice.

- Stress comes when you forget to take a step back, plan accordingly, and take each day a moment at a time.
- There is no such thing as failure. Risk big to win big!
- Find the people who lift you up, and avoid the ones who try to push you down.
- Never let the haters bring you down to their level.
- Focus on giving, not getting, and your world will be filled with love.
- Don't be afraid to be a fangirl; share your admiration and see if you can join in their endeavors.
- Your passions hold the key to your future. If you love what you do, you'll never work a day in your life.
- There is no shortcut to success except this: Work harder than everyone else, and overdeliver on every task you are given.
- Don't fear money. Commit to earning it, saving it, investing it, and asking for it. By doing so, you are paving the way for all girls, everywhere, to earn their fair share.
- Speak up often, clearly, and with conviction. Your power is in your perspective, and you can change the world when you add it to the conversation.

Love always,

Tiffany

ACKNOWLEDGMENTS

Thank you to Erin Stein, Cindy DiTiberio, Jill Grinberg, and Denise St. Pierre for your incredible belief, passion, and dedication to this book. Throughout these past two years of collaboration, I have been so grateful for your friendship and support.

Thank you to my father; my mother; my brother, David; and my sister, Kym, for your endless devotion to this project. There were so many nights when our laughter is what kept me going. I am so thankful for our loving family.

Thank you to our team at Mogul, for always offering to step up to the challenge, no matter how seemingly impossible. With our hard work, passion, and dedication, we always make the "impossible" possible.

Thank you to Chris Brizzi for your kindness and for your strength. You are always there for me. Thank you for bringing a smile to my face, always.

And most of all, thank you to the girls and women worldwide who have been with us every step of the way. We wouldn't be where we are today without you.

 **Tiffany Pham** is the founder and CEO of Mogul, one of the most influential companies for girls and women worldwide, providing information access, economic opportunity, and education. As a coder, she developed the first version of Mogul, now reaching millions across 196 countries. Tiffany was named one of *Forbes'* "30 Under 30" in media, *Business Insider's* "30 Most Important Women Under 30" in technology, *ELLE Magazine's* "30 Women Under 30 Who Are Changing the World," among many other honors. Tiffany is a judge on the TLC TV show *Girl Starter*, and co-host of the show *Positive Pushback*. She speaks at the United Nations, Microsoft, Hearst, Viacom, Bloomberg, *The New York Times*, The Wharton School, Scripps Research Institute, SXSW, and around the world. She is a graduate of Yale and Harvard Business School. Download the Mogul app or visit onmogul.com.